A LiTTLE BOOK OF

MiRROR
MAGiCK

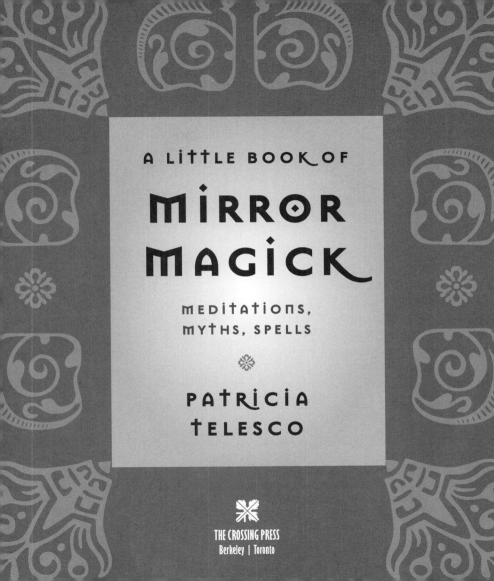

A LITTLE BOOK OF

MIRROR
MAGICK

MEDITATIONS,
MYTHS, SPELLS

❈

PATRICIA
TELESCO

❊
THE CROSSING PRESS
Berkeley | Toronto

The Crossing Press
www.crossingpress.com

A division of Ten Speed Press
P.O. Box 7123
Berkeley, California 94707
www.tenspeed.com

Distributed in Canada by Publishers Group West.

Cover and text design by Nina Barnett

Library of Congress Cataloging-in-Publication Data

Telesco, Patricia, 1960-
  A little book of mirror magick : meditations, myths, spells / Patricia Telesco.
      p. cm.
Includes bibliographical references.
  ISBN 1-58091-144-7 (pbk.)
  1. Magic mirrors. I. Title.
  BF1891.M28T45 2003
  133.4'3--dc22

2003014120

First printing, 2003

Printed in Canada

1 2 3 4 5 6 7 8 9 10—06 05 04 03

CONTENTS

6   Preface

10   Introduction

24   **Chapter 1: Scry If You Want To**
Making Your Own Magick Mirror

60   **Chapter 2: Through the Looking Glass**
The Diviner's Mirror

92   **Chapter 3: Mirror, Mirror on the Wall**

126   **Chapter 4: Reflections**
Mirror Meditations and Rituals

159   **Chapter 5: Smoke and Mirrors**
Adding Astrology or Feng Shui to Mirror Magick

189   **Appendix A**
Mirror Gods and Goddesses

195   **Appendix B**
Mirror Holidays, Festivals, Ceremonies, and Rituals

204   Bibliography

PREFACE

My mother says I must not pass too near that glass;
she is afraid that I will see a little witch that looks like me.
—Sarah Morgan Bryant Piatt

"**M**irror, mirror, on the wall, who is the fairest of them all?" In *Snow White,* the wicked witch stares into her magick mirror asking this question. The mirror then swirls with color and light, revealing the face of the fair Snow White. We find a similar bit of mirror lore in the *Arabian Nights,* where a maiden's purity was measured by the way in which her image appeared in a magick mirror. If it was clear, her heart and body were declared chaste.

While the first fairy tale portrays the witch negatively, and the second appears to use the mirror to manipulate a person's devotion, both provide a peek into an ancient magickal art: mirror scrying. For thousands of years and in a variety of cultural settings, humans have looked into mirrored surfaces hoping to find revealed the truth of the past, hidden matters in the present, and maybe even a glimpse into the elusive future.

Mirrors were also used metaphysically as charms, amulets, spell components, and a meditative focus, just to name a few possibilities. There are plenty of good illustrations of these applications.

For example, in both Europe and the United States as late as the Victorian era, covering a mirror protected the home from a visit from a recently deceased relative's spirit (amuletic value) and turning a mirror outward was said to turn away the evil eye (a kind of spell).

More commonly, people everywhere look in the mirror to primp and hone, admire and adorn the image of self reflected there. This duality of function is not unusual. In fact, the more commonplace an item, the more likely it has some use in magick. After all, our ancestors were very pragmatic: it's handy, so use it. Also, the powerful symbolism of the mirror as reflecting the true self was not lost on the ancients. Anything with such representative value and availability was bound to show up in the clever and ever resourceful witch's kit.

A Little Book of Mirror Magick builds on this rich history. Mirror magick is truly a wonderful legacy from the metaphysical world and its practices, and it has not seen much attention in a long time. We're about to change all that. In these pages, the art of mirror magick returns to your home and spiritual life in fun and functional ways. You will learn how to make your own magickal mirrors and to bless and use a variety of mirrored surfaces in and around your home. But that's only scratching the silvery surface. Throughout this book there are dozens of hands-on activities with mirrors aimed at meeting an equal variety of everyday needs—from inspiring love and prosperity to breaking a streak of bad luck.

We'll begin with the myths and superstitions surrounding mirrors. Why? Because many of these have incredibly useful insights that are easily applied to magick. For example, the Taoists say that the mirror represents self-realization—the ability to see one's true nature. An old story tells us of a book of all knowledge that, when opened, had but one page—you guessed it, a mirror. *A Little Book of Mirror Magick* helps you examine these ideas on a personal, spiritual level. Now you can look in the mirror and see the "witch" that looks like you. And you can begin considering mirrors as a great aid in all the magick that same witch wishes to whip up. As for superstition, let's just consider one well-known belief—breaking a mirror brings bad luck. Well, not if you're a crafty witch. Rather than accept the negative energy, we turn it around and find a good use for those shards. In this case, you gather up those remnants, put them in a jar, and place it somewhere to keep negativity and bad fortune away from you. This is a simple form of what's commonly called a witch bottle, and it's used for protection.

With the historical foundations firmly in place, *A Little Book of Mirror Magick* goes on to teach you not only how to make all sorts of magickal mirrors, but also how to turn them into effective tools. You'll discover how to scry (and get results), use mirrors effectively in meditation and ritual, blend mirror magick with astrology and feng shui, and even identify the gods and goddesses who can bless and empower your efforts further.

The purpose of this book is to provide you with a wealth of ideas for using any mirrored surface in your spiritual and magickal pursuits. Think about it—mirrors are everywhere. Your kitchen knife has a mirrored surface. The rearview mirror of your car will suffice. Even a piece of aluminum foil from a gum wrapper can become a handy, immediate implement to achieve whatever goal you have in your mind and heart.

So rather than continue to sit reflecting on what's to come, let's get busy and shine a light in those mirrors.

myth management

the history, legends, and folklore of mirrors

*The face is the mirror of the mind, and eyes without
speaking confess the secrets of the heart.*
—Saint Jerome

In any story, it's always good to start at the beginning. While it's tempting to skip ahead, not having all the details from the first few pages can dampen the overall effect of any book and leave you scratching your head. Similarly, in magick it's good to have solid information and get to know our potential tools and techniques inside and out. In this case, our "first page" begins with an examination of some basic mirror facts.

Mirrors are typically made of plate glass. One side of the glass is coated with metal or other reflective preparation. Between these two surfaces is what's called the "mirror line." While highly polished metals and even the surface of water can act as reflective surfaces, the glass and metal combination has been the most refined one, and thus most widely sought after for its clarity. This is the type of mirror we'll be using most widely in this book.

Three types of mirrors are commonly used in the world:

- ❀ **Plane: This has a flat surface so the rays of light that reflect off it change very little from the original character (meaning you get a more exacting result). The image in the mirror will appear to be the same distance both in front of, and behind, the mirror's surface.**
- ❀ **Convex: This mirror's surface bulges toward you, making the image smaller than reality.**
- ❀ **Concave: The word cave gives us a clue to this mirror's shape, which is akin to the inside of a hollow ball. How the image appears in a concave mirror depends on where an item is in relation to the curvature, but it will always be inverted.**

Concave and convex mirrors can be used in magick if you wish, but be sure to consider the symbolism in both the smaller image and the inverted image. For example, I might use the convex mirror for diminishing negativity and the concave one for shifting energy (turning it upside down).

HiSTORY

The first mirrors were simply surfaces that reflected images back to those peering in. Nature provided ready sources such as wells, ponds, puddles after a rain storm, and sometimes the surface of a shiny stone or crystal. As humankind's technology and skills improved, the surface of a blade became a mirror, as did pieces of armor and any other type of polished metal with a relatively flat surface. Although crude at best, highly polished disks of bronze, silver, or tin began to be carried as personal mirrors by those with the means to afford them. Here are some of the more interesting highlights in the mirror's history:

- ❀ **106–48 B.C.E.: Silver mirrors are first made by Pasiteles in the period of Pompey the Great. They quickly become more popular than bronze ones.**
- ❀ **1st century C.E.: Mirrors large enough to reflect the whole human body appear along with the increasing popularity of hand mirrors among the Celts, followed by the Romans, and in most of Europe in the Middle Ages. The most prevalent mirror is made of silver or polished bronze.**
- ❀ **4th century: Lamblichus, a Neoplatonist, describes various scrying methods in *De Mysteriis Egyptorum*, a work later used by Nostradamus.**
- ❀ **437–553: St. Remigius, archbishop of Reims, practices scrying.**
- ❀ **7th century: Silver mirrors are now almost completely replaced by glass ones.**
- ❀ **12th and 13th centuries: Mirrors are backed with metallics.**
- ❀ **14th–15th centuries: Nurnburg and Venice have established strong reputations for outstanding mirror production. At the same time in Germany, Trithemius, abbot of a monastery at Spannheim, writes definitive occult works with scrying instructions, including praying over a crystal ball for visions.**

- ❀ **1519–1589: Catherine de Medici uses a special glass to study the future. This was in the Louvre until the late 1600s, when it disappeared.**
- ❀ **16th century: Mirrors are made of glass in large quantities in Venice; Nostradamus writes about seeing visions in the spirits of fire (a type of scrying).**
- ❀ **17th century: Mirror production stretches to London and Paris for high-quality, expensive mirrors; John Dee uses mirrors for scrying in Queen Elizabeth's court; Count Cagliostro uses scrying to make various historical predictions.**
- ❀ **1800s: An early member of the Golden Dawn, Frederick Hockley, conducts various scrying experiments.**
- ❀ **1897: Miss Davy de Cusse attaches a mirror to the front of her car for the first rearview mirror.**
- ❀ **1903: The transparent mirror (a two-way mirror) is officially patented in Ohio by Emil Bloch.**
- ❀ **20th century: Aluminum is introduced as a reflecting material because of efficiency and oxidation resistance.**

From the seventeenth century onward, mirrors became more and more important for decoration. Frames were often made from ivory, ebony, silver, and tortoiseshell and then decorated further with all types of beadwork, woods, and carvings.

By the eighteenth century, painted frames became popular along with accompanying candlesticks (how very pagan). In the nineteenth century, the skills for making mirrors had improved to the point where freestanding mirrors were completely possible at a much cheaper cost. With both availability and affordability firmly in place, mirrors quickly became among the most common of household implements and remain so to this day.

It should be noted that throughout this history various cultures placed symbolic value on the mirror, each according to their era and societal beliefs. In the West, the mirror came to represent vanity and lust as well as truth (the mirror never lies). Meanwhile, among the Greeks and many people in the Middle East, it was an emblem of great goddesses like Aphrodite.

The Japanese use the mirror as an imperial, solar symbol. In Hinduism, mirrors are an emblem of enlightenment and overcoming mundane illusions. The mirror is one of the Eight Precious Things of Buddhism, and in China it represents sincerity, peace, and joy in relationships. Finally, among Christians a mirror is a metaphor for the human heart that, when polished to its most beautiful form, reflects the divine. To obtain a better understanding of where and how these various symbolic values originated, let's turn now to the global myths and legends of mirrors.

MYTH AND LEGEND

One of the most commonly known myths that centers around a person's reflection comes to us from Greece. It begins with a youth named Narcissus who was loved greatly by the nymphs. Sadly, Narcissus was cruel, and he rejected them all. In response, the nymphs prayed to the gods that Narcissus would someday come to understand how it felt to be spurned.

It was not long before the gods had a chance to respond to the nymphs' prayer. Narcissus came upon a woodland fountain where he saw an image of incredible beauty. Thinking it to be a water spirit, he fell madly in love. No matter how much he yearned, there was no response from the pond, until at last he pined away and died, leaving nothing but a purple flower where his body should have been.

On the flip side of Narcissus and his self-love, we find Perseus, the son of Zeus. This young hero traveled to Libya in an effort to kill the gorgon Medusa. To help him in his quest, he was given a finely polished shield by Hermes, which he used as a protective mirror to remain free from the gorgon's stony gaze. Once he'd captured Medusa's head, he cleverly used the magic that remained to defeat the titan Atlas, who had tried to take the golden apples from Hesperides. The shield protected Perseus from being turned to stone, and, according to the story, all that now remains of the titan is the range of mountains known as Atlas.

Not all mirror folklore is quite so positive. In Jewish tradition, mirrors are often called the Cave of Lilith. As the story goes, Lilith was the first wife of Adam. She was banished from the Garden of Eden when she refused to make herself subservient to Adam (specifically, she refused to get into the missionary position with him during sex). When she was cast out, she was made into a demon figure, and Adam was given a second wife, Eve, who was fashioned from his rib to ensure her obedience to her man.

Every mirror is a gateway to the Other World, the region that leads directly to Lilith's cave. That is the cave where Lilith went when she was cast from Adam and the Garden of Eden and where she entertained demon lovers. From these secret trysts, multitudes of demons were born. When they want to return to our realm, they simply enter the nearest mirror. That is why it is said that Lilith makes her home in every mirror.

Another tale from the *Arabian Nights* recounts how a special mirror was obtained from the king of the Jann. This mirror was specially prepared so that the prince could discern if his wife was chaste. If the maiden was pure, the mirror would show a clear image. If she was unchaste in any way, the image would be dark. This mirror was called the mirror of al-Asnam.

In Japan, the creator god known as Izanagi was said to have given his children a special mirror. The children were to kneel before this and look at it until all evil thoughts and passions dissolved. Interestingly enough, it's said that in the Shinto version of hell a giant mirror awaits new arrivals, showing them their sins. This belief is similar to Hindu tradition, in which Yama, the guardian of the underworld, uses mirrors to judge a soul's karma.

Another story from Japan is that of the sun goddess, Amaterasu. For a while, Amaterasu hid in a cave, making the world cold and dark. Another goddess coaxed her out of the cave using a magic mirror that reflected her beauty and showed what she had hidden from the world. To this day, many Shinto shrines have a mirror inside as a reminder of both these stories.

Next, we can look to a figure in the Hindu pantheon, a goddess named Nu Kua. Nu Kua appears as a serpent-dragon who came to Earth when it was separated from the heavens. She saw her reflection upon Earth's waters, and, realizing how lonely she was, she fashioned humankind after that image from the Earth's clay.

In a creation myth from Mesoamerica, we discover two beings helping to support the heavens. Quetzalcoatl and Tezcatlipoca, with assitance from other deities, raised the sky for the present world. Quetzalcoatl turned himself into a tree clothed in feathers, and Tezcatlipoca became a tree covered in divinatory mirrors (implying the all-seeing nature of this god). From that time forward, these two were known as the gods of the heavens and the stars whose dominion lies along the Milky Way.

These stories are but a sampling. Nonetheless, they reveal many of the powers the ancients believed mirrors contained, including:

❀ **Protecting and shielding (especially when turned outward toward the source of trouble)**
❀ **Serving as a meditative aid**
❀ **Forming a gateway to other realms**
❀ **Improving personal perspectives**
❀ **Future telling (divination)**
❀ **Truth seeing**
❀ **Balancing karma**
❀ **Reflecting the light of Spirit**

Our modern reflections on mirrors aren't much different. In fact, practitioners continue to use them for all these purposes.

DREAMING OF MIRRORS

In examining the various stories about mirrors, it's nearly impossible to avoid finding references to their meaning in dreams. Our dreams tell us much about humankind's perceptions—what we fear and what we honor. In turning to the world's dream lore, we find that mirrors appearing in your dreams may be interpreted as follows:

❋ In Islamic tradition, this dream portends one of six things: a woman coming into your life, a girl coming into your life, rank and dignity on the horizon, a new friend, a life or business partner, or good trade.
❋ In China, bright mirrors foretell of good fortune, a broken mirror indicates a broken marriage, and the gift of a new mirror indicates a son or daughter who will achieve great fame.
❋ A mirror is a metaphorical reflection of a specific part of your life that needs attention.
❋ A mirror represents the way you wish people would see you or a situation.
❋ Transformation is indicated, especially if the mirror breaks in the dream.
❋ Cloudy mirrors represent uncertainty.
❋ Covered mirrors symbolize some type of blockage (perhaps something in your past is haunting you).

- ❋ In Jungian psychology, mirrors represent something you're unwilling to face in total truthfulness during waking hours.
- ❋ To see others in a mirror denotes that they will act unfairly toward you to promote their own interests.
- ❋ To see animals in a mirror presages disappointment and losses in fortune.

Dream interpretation is very subjective. What a symbol means to you personally and what it means in a book can be two different things. Nonetheless, mirrors are one of those pervasive archetypes in our consciousness that we should pay attention to. While this isn't a physical mirror that you can use for magick, the symbolic value may prove important to your personal or spiritual growth and definitely in your understanding of how to better use this magickal tool.

FOLKLORE AND SUPERSTITION

Myths substantially influence human thought and behavior. Folklore and superstition work hand in hand with those myths and influence us far more than we're aware. These beliefs are often huge repositories for magickal traditions, having been a safe place to hide witchery when the general atmosphere for these arts was dangerous.

Some of the folk beliefs and traditions surrounding mirrors are more easily understood when we examine the language of a people. For example, when you realize that the Egyptian term for "mirror" meant "life," and that in India the Great Goddess was called the Mirror of the Abyss, it becomes much clearer why mirrors were valued and credited with all types of magickal attributes in those settings. The key here is that amazement toward the human reflection and the overall Spirit of the mirror was not limited to any particular global location or era. This amazement and the human fascination regarding our form have walked the world together for a long time. Let's take a quick look at some of these folk beliefs:

- ❋ Breaking a mirror brings seven years of bad luck. Breaking the image was thought to break the soul seen therein or harm the indwelling spirit and bring about its ire.
- ❋ If you do happen to break a mirror, avoid the negative fate by washing the pieces in a south-running stream or bury them to avoid bad luck. Do not, under any circumstances, gaze into the pieces. This comes from the idea that mirrors hold the key to our future and breaking one can break that future.
- ❋ Covering a mirror in a thunderstorm keeps the house safe from lightning (the spirit of the storm). Similarly, cover a mirror after a death in the home. This closes the portal to the other world.
- ❋ Keeping a baby from looking in a mirror before the age of six months avoids a life of troubles, especially those caused by mischievous spirits that might come through the mirror and influence the child.

- A mirror falling and breaking on its own foretells of death or some type of ending.
- Placing a bowl and a shiny knife behind a door in your home will keep away sorcerers because they will see their reflection and run away.
- Vampires have no soul; therefore, they have no reflection in a mirror. This idea ties into why not seeing your reflection in a mirror was said to predict serious illness or death and why Celtic women were often buried with mirrors to hold their souls firmly in place.
- Two people first seeing each other in a mirror before they date will experience a happy relationship (mirrors do not lie).
- If you wish to see the image of a future mate, eat an apple in front of a mirror and then brush your hair. Watch for an image to appear behind your shoulder (this ties into scrying).
- The reflection in the mirror is a projection of your soul. This concept was so strong that in eighteenth-century India women waved mirrors before Kali instead of performing human sacrifices and purportedly pleased the goddess nonetheless.
- Leaving a bowl of water on a grave keeps the soul in place, since its reflection will be captured in the water.

Modern-minded folk find many such beliefs a little silly. Other people, however, cling to superstitions as truths to be heeded respectfully. I'm somewhere in between these two views. Starting with the "silly" part, I believe our fate is not foreordained by any particular event or set of circumstances—how we respond is what really matters in the long haul. And while I'll be the first to admit that I find myself unconsciously following the protocol of some superstitions (like not walking under a ladder), I also have to wonder if logic and common sense don't figure heavily into that action. After all, there is a good reason not to walk under ladders from a safety standpoint (not to mention not wanting paint dropped on a new coat).

As for the crowd that follows folkways religiously, there's some merit to their perspective. I feel that any belief that has resonated in human awareness for hundreds if not thousands of years has a certain power to it. The fact that numerous people followed that folkway and honored it repeatedly in their lives puts serious energy into the mini-ritual of superstitious actions. That energy is something a clever witch can tap. If you keep this balance in mind in how, when, where, and why you use the superstitions about mirrors, you'll have the best of both worlds.

If we look at superstitions more closely, they give us a lot of clues about how to begin that tapping process. In particular, notice that these beliefs include the following processes:

- Covering a mirror to close the lines to other realms or specific energies
- Turning a mirror toward or away from something or someone
- Reusing the parts from a broken mirror to transform a negative into a positive
- Placing a mirror in a sacred space as an offering
- Applying a mirror as a charm (especially for true seeing and relationships) and gazing upon it to see the future

In the chapters that follow you'll see applications just like these, illustrating that even now we can participate in a long-loved tradition from our ancestors. Sure, we'll put some new polish on that ol' mirror and give it that magickal gleam, but all in all the customs and methods haven't changed much except where technology eases our efforts. Speaking of which, let's get started on the "crafty" portion of things—it's hard to use a magick mirror if you haven't made one first.

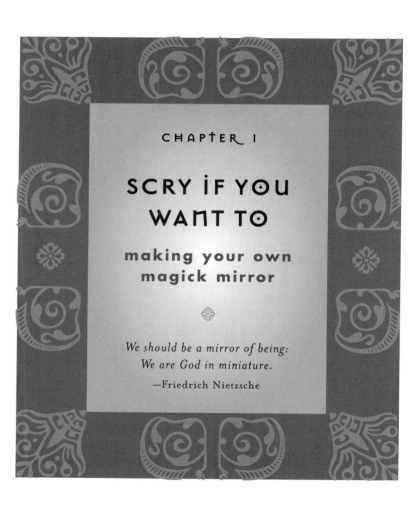

CHAPTER 1

SCRY IF YOU WANT TO

making your own magick mirror

❧

We should be a mirror of being:
We are God in miniature.

—Friedrich Nietzsche

In the sixteenth century, Swiss alchemist Paracelsus put together an elaborate formula for making a magick mirror. This process included heating lead and adding mercury, gold, silver, copper, iron filings, and dry herbs. Each ingredient had exasperatingly precise measurements, and the steps for the process were each to be performed at specific times when the planets would be most auspicious. This took several weeks, after which another appropriate time had to be chosen to polish the mirror before it would heed the wizard's questions and answer them.

I find this process very interesting as it speaks of ritual magick and folklore all in one historical tidbit. About the only item that seems odd to me is the use of iron, since so many magickal creatures (like fairy folk) were thought banished or restrained by the substance. Perhaps that was the whole idea—to keep unwanted spirits from tinkering with the outcome. Thankfully, our processes need not be so complex.

MAGICK VS. THE MUNDANE

In order to make an effective magick mirror, you first need to understand what it is that sets this implement apart from the one in your bathroom. It boils down to the skill, focus, and willpower of the witch or mage who constructs it. Without that energy flow, a mirror is just, well, a mirror. Mirrors are fascinating and entrancing, but they are without that special life that the spark of magick provides.

Are magickally produced mirrors alive in the sense that we are? Not exactly, and this depends heavily on the manner in which one makes the mirror. For example, in shamanic traditions the item being used as a mirror, such as a highly polished stone, might be fed with blood to keep it energized.

Instead of using blood, some European wise men called upon spirits to inhabit their mirrors and aid in a mirror's accuracy. Thus, an indwelling spirit gives the tool a kind of life all its own until that spirit is released. While this method is very ancient, I have some serious ethical issues with commanding any spirit. It breaks the rule of not hindering free will. If a spirit is asked and accepts the "job," that's different, but to simply be pressed into servitude hardly makes for a happy camper. Since this is not a technique I personally use or one to which I subscribe, I won't be discussing it much here. Rather, I will leave it to your own sensibilities to determine if you want to explore spirit capture further.

An alternative approach along these lines that's functional and far more sensible is that of giving the mirror an elementary spirit. Rather than a spirit that's been commanded and entrapped, an elementary is a personally devised energy form. In fact, it's a miniature elemental with a life span, purpose, and rudimentary personality that would use the mirror as a "body" or home. We'll discuss how to go about doing this later in this chapter under Elemental Mirrors.

With or without an indwelling spirit, a properly contrived magick mirror works both in this world and in the astral. While all things have a presence in the astral world, not everything *functions* in that realm. Once created, blessed, consecrated, and empowered, the mirror opens that doorway to the user. It can be used to communicate with individuals or spirits over vast distances (with individuals, typically several mirrors are created—all of which are identical). It can become a window into time, and it can be an effective amulet or ritual tool. Better still, the mirror can be turned "on" and "off" as needed, thereby conserving energy.

Any implement that has such a diversity of applications also has some caveats. In particular, I recommend that you use a protected sacred space when your mirror is active. Like a ouija board, the mirror creates a bridge between realities (a portal, if you will). You'll want the capacity to safeguard that portal from unwanted company (who may or may not have your best interest at heart). A sample approach to creating sacred space in which to use your mirror will be covered in chapter 2.

when a mirror is not a mirror

No, this isn't some type of riddle. Before getting into a more formal process for making various magickal mirrors, I want to point out that many reflective objects were used by our ancestors when no actual mirror was available. On their list we find things like polished coal, a black glass bowl, and a slice of obsidian. Similarly, there are simple items around your house that could work as a mirror if you're in a pinch. When we consider for a moment that the original magick mirrors were things like pools of water or reflective blades, we certainly have a long history of creativity on our side. In fact, even in the 1300s various members of the church complained that clergy still used polished steel surfaces to "consult with spirits."

Just walking around my home today, I found several surfaces had enough reflectivity to function in scrying, and some are small enough to become spell and ritual components too. Here are just a few:

- Silverware (knife and spoon back in particular)
- TV and computer screens (turned off)
- Stapler back
- Glass doors on cabinets
- Plastic surfaces with a smooth finish
- Metal measuring cups
- Black ink poured into a cup or other holder
- Cooled wax
- Polished cabochons (in particular obsidian)

I'm sure I've overlooked a few things, so take a moment to peer around the room you're in and walk through the rest of the house. See what you can find.

Whenever you're in dollar stores and other bargain outlets, grab a few small mirrors that you can prepare and carry with you. No one said that magick had to cost a fortune to work perfectly well, and I am very much an advocate of keeping spirituality within one's budget. About the only caveat here is that it's prudent to take the time to cleanse any items you find at these stores and even those around your home. A lot of people handle them daily, and thus they can pick up residual energy that may hinder your efforts.

Simple forms of cleansing include washing with lemon juice and water, sprinkling with salt, or moving the item through a purgative smoke like sage or cedar. Another easy method is visualization. Hold the item in both hands. In your mind's eye imagine the bright white light of Spirit pouring down over you (this may feel slightly warm or tingly). Now let that energy flow over and into the item you're holding. Continue until it feels squeaky clean.

As for using these items, just look at the surface as you would a crystal ball or any other magickal mirror. In particular, TV and computer screens work incredibly well because your mind already anticipates seeing images on them. With an item like a spoon, it often helps to dab a bit of olive oil on the surface. This creates a slight blur that may help your eyes unfocus. We'll discuss more specific instructions on scrying in chapter 2.

the mirror of you

Before going further into the process of making magickal mirrors, let's pause to talk about self-preparation. The creation of any magickal tool should be a well-considered endeavor. It's not something to just slap together without a little bit of introspection and preparation. In particular, make sure you're not ill, angry, or out of balance in any way when you're working on the mirror. Even the most adept witch knows that it's hard to shield yourself when these conditions exist, and you don't want any bad vibes going into this tool.

If all seems to go well with your self-check, step two is to consider the tool itself. For what function is this mirror intended? Does the process you have for making it include the proper components and words to support that function? Review the steps provided, make personally meaningful adaptations, get the ingredients you need, and then set everything aside for just a few minutes longer.

The last step is to cleanse yourself and shift your focus from mundane matters to magickal ones. At the very least, wash your hands in soap and water before handling the mirror's components. If you can take a full shower and dab yourself with a favorite anointing oil, all the better. Other things you might want to consider doing beforehand include:

❀ **Creating a spiritually positive working environment with candles, incense, or music**
❀ **Donning a special item of clothing or jewelry**
❀ **Praying, meditating, chanting, dancing, or drumming**

What's most important here is that whatever steps you take at this juncture should improve your focus and put you in the right frame of mind for what's ahead.

SiMPLE SCRYiNG MiRRORS

Before I go into various processes for making simple scrying mirrors, I'd like to allay one magickal myth. While the ancients felt the cost of the components used in making a magickal tool somehow indicated that tool's power, I tend to disagree. In my opinion, just because something is fairly easy to make at a reasonable cost doesn't mean it lacks power. In fact, the personal energy that goes into making the item and the thoughtfulness behind it seem to improve the results across the board. So if anyone tries to tell you that something is too simple or cheap to work—respond with a hearty "bah."

On the other hand, if you want a fancy mirror and it would be more meaningful to you, that's another matter. Ultimately, whenever you're considering creating a spiritual implement, you need to ask yourself how this item will be used, what it means to you symbolically, and what personalization you want to bring into the procedure. In the end, you want something that really sings the song of your soul and vibrates with positive, personal energy. So it's okay to go fancier; I'd just rather give you the basics and let you embellish as your spirit dictates.

Let's begin with what I consider the easiest mirror to make:

1. First, you'll need a glass picture frame. The frame can be any size, shape, and material you wish, but a lot of people say that darker frames make the scrying process easier. If you want, get several

frames in various sizes and shapes that can be used for a variety of magickal purposes. For example, a leafy or green-toned frame might be fun to make with attuning to Earth energies and animal spirits in mind. Or, a round wooden frame into which you've carved elemental symbols could become a tool for your ritual space. I've found that a lot of department stores have wonderful frames for between $3 and $20, depending on how big a surface you want. I've even gotten pewter-toned ones for $1 on sale. Try Goodwill, flea markets, garage sales, and swap meets and you can get them for even less than that.

2. Buy a can of high-gloss black enamel spray paint. Alternatively, I've had some success using very, very dark green or very dark purple. Read the label and make sure the paint is suitable for glass. Hobby shops, hardware stores, and many department stores carry spray paint in the craft supply section.

3. Take the glass out of the frame and clean it, making sure you don't leave any lint behind. Let it dry for at least an hour. Also clean off the frame and consider cleansing it spiritually by moving it through sage or cedar incense. A lot of people have probably handled this item at the store, and you want to start with a pure component into which you can place your energies.

4. Place the glass on a cardboard surface larger than the size of the glass (this protects your work area from spray paint). Remember to pick up the glass by the edges so you don't get fingerprints on it again. If you feel you want some type of symbol behind the paint, this is the point at which to add one. You can do this using a specially chosen paint, but try to keep it from becoming thick or the surface of your mirror will be lumpy.

5. Spray paint the glass using even strokes. Cover the glass completely, taking care that the paint doesn't run. If you're working outdoors, winds can cause this and also sometimes blow debris into the paint. This paint must dry completely before you do a second coat. Some people prefer just one coat of paint; others seem to favor two or three, so you might have to experiment a bit. If you want to add a little fine glitter (like body glitter) into the paint, now is the time to gently blow it onto the surface. I like to use opalescent, as the effect is beautiful in candlelight. For those of you who have trouble scrying with a plain black surface, the glitter gives your eyes something on which to catch and often helps the process along.

6. Put the glass back into the frame, glass side out (again, watch your fingerprints).

7. If you wish, take a piece of lint-free, natural-fiber cloth and place it over the top. The covering of the mirror is akin to shutting a door. It leaves the mirror in a nonactive mode until needed.

8. Finally, at some juncture before you start using the mirror, you should bless and charge it. I'll go into various ways of handling this process later in this chapter.

If you'd like to get a little fancier, you could begin by making your own frame. You can also consider additives for the mirror's surface preparation that are technically called fluid condensers. The purpose behind the fluid condenser (which may or may not be an actual liquid) is to increase the chi or overall magnetic energy working in and around the mirror. This energy mixes and mingles with the human aura for amplification. Here's a list of some of the things typically used for this purpose (often in a blend of six or more, but in minute quantities):

- Eggshell
- White feather (or feather from a water-dwelling bird)
- Spiderwebs
- Your hair
- Seashells
- Salt
- Silver filings
- Quartz
- Rose petals (white)
- Willow sawdust
- Tincture of moss, mugwort, or other lunar herbs

Other secondary condensers that have been recommended in various books include elder flower, willow, jasmine, water lily, poppy, cinnamon, bay, orange, marigold, tobacco, vervain, oak, clover, pine, sage, lavender, and chamomile.

In the case of the larger items, you'll need to find a way to pulverize them. The finer you can make the powder, the better. Sift out any shards for an even consistency, then sprinkle just a little over the surface of your mirror. For extra symbolism, move your hand clockwise around the frame as you release the blend to encourage a positive flow of energy. Remember, however, that you may need to coat your mirror more than once to get a smooth surface when using powdered condensers.

An alternative to this is making a tincture from your chosen components. This can be accomplished by steeping the chosen items in rainwater or spring water. The proportions are up to you; however, take care that the energies of the herbs are carefully balanced with each other. Let everything come to a low simmer and continue cooking until the liquid reduces by at least one third. Some ritualists add gold tincture to this foundation, but it's costly and not easy to find. I consider it optional for both reasons.

As with the powdered condenser, sprinkle the tincture evenly over the mirror; then apply your paint after it dries. The obvious advantage here is having a smooth, finished surface for your mirror.

CABALISTIC MIRRORS

Cabalists have been known to make themselves a set of mirrors for scrying, each of which is inscribed with a planetary symbol and used for one specific day of the week. For example, a moon mirror made from polished silver with the symbol of the moon etched upon it would be consulted only on Monday, the moon's day. The rest of the week goes as follows:

TUESDAY made from iron and marked with the symbol for Mars

WEDNESDAY made from mercury and marked with Mercury's sign

THURSDAY made of tin and marked with Jupiter's sign

FRIDAY made of copper and etched with an image of Venus

SATURDAY made of lead and marked with Saturn's sign

SUNDAY made of gold and marked with an emblem of the sun

It might seem nearly impossible to make something like this yourself, but with a little adaptation I think it's quite possible and financially plausible. Rather than make an actual gold mirror, use high-gloss gold paint on a glass surface and etch it with a symbol of the sun before it dries completely (or prepaint the image on the surface before doing your final flat coat). Similarly, use iron-colored paint for Tuesday, and so forth.

As you make your mirrors on the days of the week for which they'll be used, don't forget to add in ritualistic overtones to help you focus your mind and energies. Consider burning incense that matches the mirror's function or planetary ruler. Here are some correspondences to which to refer if you want to add this element:

SUN bay, cedar, cinnamon, marigold

MOON coconut, jasmine, lemon, lily

MERCURY bergamot, lavender, lemon verbena, marjoram

VENUS apple, cherry, hyacinth, rose

MARS basil, ginger, mint, pine
JUPITER anise, clove, nutmeg, sage
SATURN comfrey, morning glory, pansy

These aromatics could be used as part of anointing or blessing oils for yourself or your mirror too.

Besides adding incense, you can burn candles, chant, pray, play spiritually uplifting music, wear special clothing, and so on. Here's a list of the planetary colors for your reference. Use the color correspondence in choosing the color to paint each day's mirror or the colors for your candles and clothing.

SUN red, pink, gold, bright yellow, orange
MOON silver and white (also silvery blue)
MERCURY dark green and grassy hues
VENUS royal blue, pure white, opalescent
MARS all shades of red
JUPITER yellow
SATURN brown, blackish blue, generally dark colors

Basically, you want this whole process to keep your mind and spirit focused on the goal. The more multisensual your technique becomes, the more energy it produces because you're responding and opening up on many different levels of awareness.

Once the mirrors are made, how do you use this system correctly? To my mind, the best approach is gearing your questions toward the overall energies of a particular day. Here's a list of correspondences for the subjects over which each day of the week rules:

MONDAY spiritual progress, fertility, growth, creativity, intuition, the goddess

TUESDAY logic, reason, conscious thought, skill, legal questions, learning, health

WEDNESDAY inventiveness, resourcefulness, insightfulness, originality

THURSDAY energy, zeal, dedication, honor, loyalty, longevity, obligations, power

FRIDAY all relationships, matters of love, effectiveness, communication

SATURDAY outcomes, resolutions, cause and effect, motivation, perception, judgment

SUNDAY knowledge, education, truthfulness, leadership, authority

To put this information into an example, if you had a question about how trustworthy someone was, you might consult Thursday's mirror (on Thursday, of course). Or, if you wanted more insight into a potential relationship, you'd consult Friday's mirror.

ELEMENTAL MIRRORS

The elements of Earth, Air, Fire, and Water are important to magickal practices. When the symbolic values and attributes of these powers are used effectively, they become the backbone upon which much of our magick rests. It seems reasonable that a practitioner might wish to create elemental mirrors that honor those powers and, in turn, end up with a highly refined tool.

A German manuscript from the 1600s talks about an Earth mirror that was created simply by placing mirrored glass about two inches above a paper or wooden surface on which a question was written. To open the mirror, the mage placed salt in his mouth (purification), prayed, made sacred signs over the mirror, and then breathed upon it (giving life). I am not completely sure why this was called an Earth mirror, because the use of vital breath would seem to make it more of an Air-oriented tool.

Thus, I would recommend following that simple process to energize an Air mirror and repeating it just before using the mirror for spells or scrying. Note, however, that any question you pose to an elemental mirror should be suited to that element's personality. In this case, the dominion of Air includes imagination, education, creativity, new ideas, luck, revelation, motivation, transformation, whimsy, and hopefulness. The attributes of the other elements are as follows:

FIRE surmounting obstacles, purification, passion, power, zeal, protection, release, truth, enlightenment, banishing

WATER intuition, instinct, empathy, cleansing, sensitivity, health and wellness, fertility, generative energy, psychic and spiritual attunement, growth, slow and steady change

EARTH financial matters, abundance, consistency, dedication, foundations, tenacity, common sense, practicality, well-grounded solutions

If you're looking for an alternative way of making and empowering an Air mirror, I'd begin with the simple mirror process discussed previously, choose a paint color that matches the element (pale yellow is one option), and put a symbol for Air in the center of the mirror's surface. Once you're finished painting it, take it outside and make sure the surface is exposed to all four directional winds (you can find out which way the wind is blowing by checking the weather report). Obviously, it may take a few days to achieve a full four-wind blessing, but the symbolic value is quite powerful to my mind.

Next, let's consider a Water mirror. The simplest Water mirror begins with a stoneware or clay bowl. Paint the interior of your bowl in midnight blue-purple (perhaps with a little dark green) so it looks like the depths of the ocean. Bless the mirror (as discussed later this chapter) and then simply fill it with water from a live source such as a stream or spring. Hold the bowl in your left hand and drop a bit of ink or wax on the surface of the water. Observe the patterns in the water, wax, and ink until all stop moving. If you plan to use the Water mirror as part of a spell or ritual, simply fill it with water or pour out the water as appropriate to your goal.

There are two other historical methods of making a Water-oriented mirror that I discovered in my research. The first comes to us through a turn-of-the-century occultist named Grillot de Givry. Rather than consisting simply of water, this method uses three bowls—a red or copper one filled with an oil; a white, silver, or glass one filled with water; and a green or earthenware one filled with wine. Behind and to the right of each bowl is a candle. The bowls and candles should be shielded from light for three full days, and the weather must be totally calm for three days before using them.

The instructions go on to say that you should wear white and cover all but your eyes with a red cloth made of natural fiber. When you gaze into each bowl, you'll be shown specific time frames. The bowl with wine is the present; the bowl with oil is the past; and the bowl with water, the future. This illustration is important from two perspectives. First, it's easy to re-create these mirrors today. Secondly, the method reminds us that any liquid may represent the Water element. This, in turn, gives us greater flexibility with our components.

The third Water mirror I discovered was nothing more than a cup into which some water was poured and a coin placed inside. The coin was typically polished silver or gold. This provided extra reflectivity for the scryer. The custom also rather interestingly ties into the belief in water spirits, such as those in wishing wells. By putting the coin in the water, the diviner paid the water spirit for its aid in seeing the future.

The Fire mirror will be energized by sunlight and candlelight. I suggest a handheld mirror for this project because it makes the energizing process easier to control. Returning to our simple mirror construction, you'll want gold-tone paint for this mirror and an emblem of the sun in the middle of the glass. Hobby shops carry metallic-colored paints. If you can afford it, you could also make this mirror with gold leaf, which is quite lovely.

When the mirror is fully dry, charge it by laying it in the light of the noonday sun for several hours (how long is up to you—the key is to sense that the mirror has been saturated with that light energy). Afterward, light a yellow, orange, or gold-toned candle. Holding the mirror's handle with a towel or pot holder, move the candle clockwise around the edge of the mirror, letting the flame dance on the frame. This is an excellent time to recite an incantation, repeating it as many times as necessary until you've warmed the entire mirror's edge. Here's one example:

Fire without, fire within
By my will the magick begins
The fires of life, the fires of light
Let nothing be hidden from my sight
Spirit of spark, spirit of fire

Raise the energies ever higher
By the glow of the candle and the shine of the sun
This mirror is blessed, the work is done!
So be it.

To make a Fire mirror that can function with fire inside it, start with a freestanding incense burner or brazier. You'll need to use a heat-resistant paint like that used on barbecue grills for the inside, and if you can find it in gold, that would be best. Black isn't a color that works well to represent Fire's energy. Or, if you can find a brass incense burner you're all set.

You can use this tool with or without fire in it. Bless it much as you did the first Fire mirror; then use the reflective surface for scrying. Or, put a little bit of wood or coals inside and observe the behavior of the fire. While this second method comes more under the category of pyromancy, it's still tied into the original mirrored surface that you've created and empowered. Also, don't forget to use it on your altar as a symbol of Fire, for burning incense, and so on.

ELEMENTARY MIRRORS

Earlier in this chapter I spoke of the possibility of using an elemental mirror as a home for an elementary. Let's take a closer look at how to accomplish that task.

1. If you've created an elemental mirror, you already have an environment suitable for your elementary. The next step is to prepare your space so it honors the being you're about to birth. Bring in candles, incense, and other decorations that vibrate on the same elemental frequency as the being you're designing. And don't forget personal touches like dressing in blue to welcome a Water spirit or going barefoot when making an Earth spirit.

2. Find something keyed to the element in question and bring it into the sacred space—ashes for the Fire mirror, your tears for a Water mirror, a feather or fan for the Air mirror, or some soil from near your home for an Earth mirror.

3. This is the time to call the watchtowers if you wish to safeguard your energy until this energy you're creating is ready to take on life of its own.

4. Hold the chosen component in your hands, focus your will, and visualize the elementary forming. For Fire, the image might be that of a small spark or salamander-type creature (it will not burn you—you're its maker). The Air elementary typically has wings; the Earth spirit some type of flower, roots, or leaves; and the Water spirit appears somewhat like a tiny mermaid. This, however, is only how I perceive them—your imagery may vary.

5. Project your energy, maintaining your focus and will until you sense the presence of a little personality in the room with you. You will suddenly know you're no longer alone.

6. Breathe gently into your hands three times while visualizing it filled with the light of the Cosmos. Say the word *live*. This is a command, so mean what you say.

7. Name your elementary. This is vital because you'll use that name to call upon it in the mirror.

8. Give your elementary its purpose in detail. Be specific.

9. Give the elementary a life span. If you plan to use it in the mirror forever, it should live as long as do you.

10. Tell the elementary to live in the mirror. Place your chosen components in your hand upon the mirror's surface to make the empathic connection.

11. Take a pinch of your chosen component and put it into a charm bag or power pouch to keep you connected with this being.

12. Cover the mirror in black silk when it's not in use so the elementary rests quietly and so you're not distracted by your connection to it.

Once this mirror is completed, it becomes a personalized tool that should be prized for its intimacy and meaningfulness. Although elementary beings are less powerful than the Guardians, they are still formidable children who are eager to help you. They will not, however, typically respond to other people positively unless you've made that part of the program. Keep your elementary mirror in a place of honor away from stray hands. Remember to commune periodically with your elementary so it doesn't get lonely. And when it does its tasks correctly, a little thank you goes a long way. Even as a rudimentary life, each elementary has some level of emotion. The more you commune, appreciate, and connect with it, the better your results become.

WELLNESS MIRRORS

Because our ancestors associated the image in a mirror with the soul, it's not surprising to find mirrors being used in folk healing practices. A beautifully simple approach comes to us from India. To try this you'll need a finely polished silver bowl or basin. Fill it with water and hold it beneath the full moon. Next, look into the water and relax. Drink the lunar-charged water from the reflective bowl to aid in healing.

Here I'd like to remind you that old customs can be affected by our modern way of life. Please be careful that there is no chemical silver polish on whatever implement you use. Also, paint the inside of a cup or bowl with a material that's safe to eat off. In a pinch, I've lined a cup with aluminum foil that's been carefully smoothed.

By way of personalization, you might want to time this endeavor with a waning moon to improve the symbolic value—so sickness diminishes. If you're feeling really creative, fill the cup or bowl with a healthy herbal tea, like ginseng, rather than plain water. This way you can internalize both the moon's blessing and the helpful energies and attributes of the tea. And, depending on the size of the item used, you can carry it with you afterward as a health charm.

If you'd like to have something small to use specifically for portable protection, look in stores for a silver teacup charm, a miniature picture frame (in this case you'd be painting the glass silver rather than black to maintain continuity), or even perhaps the mirror or cup from a dollhouse set. I like using a cup because it honors the original idea of drinking the water to internalize the mirror's power. With the smaller size, you could put some of Bach's Flower Essence in the cup, bless it by moonlight, and drink it just the same.

AMULETIC AND PROTECTIVE MIRRORS

Since we're on the subject of protective mirrors, let's look at other ways of creating amulets, charms, and talismans using a mirrored surface as our fundamental component. From the time of the Greek myth of Perseus, there's certainly been a long-standing tradition of using all manner of mirrors and mirrored surfaces as protective devices. Also, mirrors were once used for signaling to people across distances—the reflective light communicating in code. So, there's no reason not to use this symbolism for magick.

While I will be providing sample applications in chapter 4, it's good to know a few basic processes from the start. Let me share with you a little about the differences between the various forms of portable magick because these differences influence your creation techniques. In particular, let's examine charms, amulets, and talismans, all of which are still in popular use.

Charms were probably the first form of spellcraft. Traditionally, a charm needed nothing more than specific words to make it work. Typically, these words rhymed or had a musical quality (the root word for charm, *carmen,* means song). The main focus for charms was that of improving good luck in various areas of life or avoiding dangers.

Over time, charms ceased to be simply words and were transformed into small valuable objects, such as crystals or rings, which were empowered by words. The little tokens for charm bracelets found at jewelry stores are a remnant of that custom. We could energize a small mirrored surface with a specific set of words repeated a symbolic number of times, so if you were making a mirror to protect a new project that you've entered into with a friend, repeating your incantation twice seems apt.

If you're unfamiliar with numeric correspondences, here's a list to which to refer:

1 unity, God, the sun, inception, focus

2 partnership, balance, awareness, the senses (touch and vision), friendship, the waxing moon

3 the triune goddess, body-mind-spirit, fortune, truth, enlightenment

4 the elements, winds, the Earth, crossroads, time, overcoming problems, abundance, growth

5 marriage, pilgrimage, versatility, insight, sacred duties, meditation

6 love, fertility, protection, dedication, productivity, completion, diligence, devotion

7 Spirit, worship, wisdom, harmony, diversity, synchronicity, metaphysical understanding, the moon

8 energy, rebirth, justice, positive transformation, increasing power, personal characteristics

9 divinatory efforts, magical mastery, psychic energy, universal law, community service, kindness

10 completeness, change, following through, listening to instinct (inner voice)

11 emotions

12 zodiacal energy, work, fruitfulness, self-sacrifice, purity

13 tenacity, patience, faith, perseverance

Amulets are similar to charms. Considering the word *amulet* means "a charm," you can see why there might be similarity. The key differences between the two boil down to function, the periodic addition of drawn emblems, and the fact that an amulet's power doesn't come to bear until a situation awakens that energy. This means that the overall charge in an amulet tends to last longer than charms. Like a battery, the less it's turned on, the longer the amulet lasts.

Generally, an amulet was designed to protect the bearer from evil or to remedy a problem and, as with the charm, the chosen object was empowered with words. To this foundation a mage might add a drawing while incanting (the drawing being representative of the amulet's function). She might also work during a propitious moon phase or planetary hour.

If you return to the section on cabalistic mirrors, you'll see an excellent example of adding a drawing to the mirror creation process. While such imagery is not necessary to the amulet's function, it does help hone the energy therein. Thus, if you decide to add a symbol to these types of mirrors, please take time to research what might be the best and most meaningful one to employ.

And what of talismans? Again, they bear a lot of similarity to amulets and charms. The talisman was always created during auspicious astrological times, using metals or gems that were inscribed with imagery. The base metal or gem and the imagery corresponded to the mage's overall goal for the piece. The key difference is that where the charm has background energy and the amulet waits to be activated, the talisman is "on" all the time and is even considered an active participant in magick. For example, one could make a mirrored wand to use in casting the magick circle as a talisman of safety. Take metallic silver paint, or silver leaf, and apply it to the wand so the end result is a reflective surface. I suggest wood as a base, perhaps chosen for its magickal significance. What woods have been special to magickal folk? Here are just a few:

ASH a favorite wood for Druidical wands

BIRCH favored for its goddess energies

HAWTHORN for fairy and wish magick

HAZEL an amulet for wisdom

PINE or nature and fertility magick

ROWAN for protection

WILLOW favored for witch's brooms

Once you've chosen the wood, the next step is to find a fallen branch. It's not a good idea to harvest a branch from a living tree because the break point can open the tree to insects or disease. Remove the bark carefully and sand the wood smooth; then apply your paint or leafing. When this is complete, the mirrored surface reflects away any unwanted energy and the tool remains as a perfectly useful casting device.

mirroring the moon

I ran across a unique procedure that used a silk hanky, a handheld mirror, and a body of water. A pond or other living water source was preferred. People often did this at Yule or the New Year specifically to determine how long it would be before finding a mate.

Sit with your back to the water. Hold the mirror in your strong hand and angle it so you can see both the moon in the sky and its reflection on the water. Next, with your other hand hold the handkerchief up over your eyes (you'll be able to see through it to the mirror). The resulting image will be distorted. You may see one moon in the mirror or several. The number of moons equates to the number of days, weeks, months, or years before finding a mate (or it could equate to any other topic in which a time frame was desired).

I think you could switch the key focus here (the moon) and use sunlight. The sun would relate better to more cognitive questions—legal issues, study, leadership, choices, and so on. The handkerchief will protect your eyes from direct sunlight. This method is best used for questions that require a numerically oriented answer. Alternatively, you can use the symbolic value of the number of images seen as indicative of your answer (see numeric correspondences under the subject of amuletic and protective mirrors in this chapter).

CONSECRATING AND CHARGING YOUR MIRROR

Depending on the mage you consulted, the exact how-to's of consecration varied. For example, in the sixteenth century the recommended procedure included buying the mirror and burying it in a grave for three weeks so spirits could inhabit the glass. Next, the actual "awakening" of the mirror would take place during the first, eighth, fifteenth, or twenty-second hour of Tuesday (hours associated with Mars). Alternatively, it would be soaked for three weeks in baptismal water remaining from a firstborn son; then the water was poured over a grave while incanting verses from Revelations. Finally, the mage would command that nothing on Earth or in heaven be hidden from his eyes.

This particular approach is interesting because we see how magick and Christianity were still mixing and mingling, especially among ritual magicians. Nonetheless, I suspect it's not an approach most modern practitioners would find appealing or inspiring. Another idea from the same era, however, works nicely with modern practices, namely, that of anointing the mirror with an herbal oil.

Anointing has long been a means of blessing in many religious traditions. In this case, the oil actually serves two purposes: the herbs in the oil (chamomile, rosemary, thyme, and cinnamon) are specifically chosen for their psychic-enhancing abilities, thereby providing a subtle energetic aromatherapy, and the oil creates a hazy surface that makes it easier to unfocus your eyes.

Creating your anointing oil isn't difficult. First, choose up to four herbs. These herbs should somehow honor the mirror you've made and its function. For example, if you make an Earth mirror (see the section on elemental mirrors), the best herbs might be those with an Earth correspondence combined with those for divination. Why only four? Unless you're a somewhat accomplished cook or herbalist, mixing more herbs than that can often yield unpleasant results.

To make your anointing oil, take one cup of good-quality olive oil and warm it in a nonaluminum pan. Place one teaspoon of each herb in a tea ball or a piece of mesh and steep it until you get a heady aroma. Cool this and store it in a dark, airtight jar away from sunlight. Dab it on both your mirror and your third eye before you begin your magickal efforts.

Oil is not the only way to bless and energize your mirror, by any means. I like to breathe on my mirrors three times before I use them for the first time and then say a brief prayer of blessing. Breath equates to life, and three is the number of body, mind, and spirit working harmoniously together. Anytime you feel your mirror needs a little energy boost, I've found this approach quite helpful. It also helps key the mirror to your unique energy signature.

Another approach is leaving the mirror in moonlight. Because the first mirrors were typically surfaces of water, and water is related to the moon, mirrors also became associated with the lunar sphere. Similarly, a witch's powers have also been connected with the moon. About the only time you might not want to use this technique is when making a Fire, sun, or Mars mirror, for which such a blessing would be in opposition to the energy desired.

To bless and energize your mirror by moonlight, begin by taking it outside on the three nights of the full moon (for the fullness of power). If weather does not permit being outdoors, find a clear window where you can sit comfortably and remain undisturbed. Next, dab the mirror with a mugwort tincture. Why mugwort? Mugwort is a lunar herb that's been used for hundreds of years in blessing and energizing mirrors, probably because of its association with the lunar goddess, Diana. Also, mugwort harvested on St. John's Eve was said to protect the user from spirits and improve the sight (both physically and spiritually). It seems ideally suited to this implement.

On each of the three nights, sit beneath the moonlight with the mirror. Meditate on the energies of that sphere and draw them into yourself. When you feel wholly connected, introduce the mirror to the moon by raising it up to the heavens much as you might lift a child. Draw the same energy into the mirror that you've brought to yourself. Now bring the mirror down and touch it to your forehead and heart chakra. The third eye chakra improves the psychic rapport between you and your mirror and creates an astral line of power connecting the tool to you personally. The heart chakra encourages you to use your implement with pure intent, that is, in perfect love.

This is an excellent time to chant, pray, or incant something personal over the mirror. If you have a god or goddess whom you follow, ask for a blessing. Afterward, sit with the mirror in your lap so both your reflection and that of the moon can be seen. Sense the connectedness between the three. Rub the frame of the mirror with the oil in your skin. Caress it. Mark it with your energy.

On the third night, carefully cover the mirror in natural cloth and put it away for future use. If possible, wait until the next waxing moon cycle before using the tool. This gives the mirror's energy time to settle and take root. It also gives you a chance to switch gears spiritually.

A third approach to blessing and charging your mirror is through visualization. In this, you'll allow silver-white energy from above (Spirit) to pour down through your crown chakra into your hands and out into the mirror. If you're making an elemental mirror, add a secondary color of light to support that element (such as blue and white for a Water mirror or red and white for a Fire mirror). Continue the visualization until it seems as if the light energy in your mind's eye is reflecting off the mirror's surface. This means it has accepted as much as it can. The beauty of this method is that it's easily repeated nearly anytime, anywhere, with no one being remotely aware of what you're doing.

Remember, magick like this takes a lot of personal energy. No matter what approach you've taken to blessing and charging the mirror, from that point forward try to make using this tool a regular part of your spiritual routine. The more you do, the more the mirror will respond to you, especially in scrying (see chapter 2). And by the way, if you ever feel your mirror is losing its edge psychically, you can use this method to fill up its spiritual battery, if you will, at any interval necessary.

the off switch?

You can give your mirror activating words. The key words act like the on-off switch for your tool, similar to the way in which opening and closing a Circle generate and dissipate a specific energy form. The beauty of power words is that they're simple and effective and have all the symbolic value necessary for working harmoniously with the mirror's magickal processes. The words I chose were "open" and "close," accompanied by hand movements akin to opening and closing a curtain. To me, that's what the mirror does—it moves aside the veil between realities and lets us look in. If you would like to give your mirrored surface command words, choose words that are meaningful to you and, if you wish, add movement. The first time you use the tool, whisper the command for "on" into the surface of the mirror thrice, then begin your scrying effort. When you're finished, whisper the "off" word three times and cover the mirror. After the first time, you will need to use your power word only once to turn the switch.

While this seems like a simple procedure, it's important and a good safety precaution. Your mirror is a gateway. It's not prudent to leave every door and window in a home open to strangers. Similarly, leaving your mirror "open" could invite unwanted energies and guests into your space. The command words avoid that issue altogether.

WORKING WITH YOUR MIRROR

The chapters that follow will give you ideas about effectively working with your new magickal tool based on the specific process you're undertaking. However, these general rules of thumb will help you no matter what your methods.

- Keep your mirror's surface clean. This helps avoid distraction and also implies that your tool is purified so energy can flow freely.
- Focus on your mirror's function from start to finish. Always understand what role your mirror will play in the magick you're making.
- Recharge or bless the mirror if it seems to begin working poorly after a while.
- Work at night during a full moon. This seems to improve the overall effect for many people (especially when scrying), but this is not an edict.
- Burn incense to heighten spiritual or psychic awareness while you work.
- Turn off all lights or dim them, except for whatever candles you've chosen (if any). Note: This isn't necessarily true if you're not using a speculum (the old word for eyeglasses).
- Remember that any images you "see" forming in the mirror really happen in your mind's eye. Focusing too much on the mirror's surface can seriously hamper results, especially in scrying.

STORAGE

When your chosen or personally made mirror is completed, you'll want to keep it safe. Most people who use their mirror regularly prefer not to let other individuals handle or use the tool. It's like giving anyone who asks the keys to your front door—it's simply not wise considering the personal energy this implement contains. Also, random handling can skew the patterns of power within the object so it won't respond as well until you cleanse it again. This is where designing your mirror with a cloth cover or having a special, safe spot in which to store it comes in handy.

When you put the mirror away after use, I strongly suggest using some type of padded box to avoid breakage. Avoid large temperature changes too. These can cause your mirrored surfaces to expand or contract and potentially break.

* * *

The ideas I've presented here are those that I've found helpful to me or are those shared by friends. If you like these ideas and a process works out nicely for you, I'd suggest transferring notes about it into your little black book so you can refer to it later (see page 83). On the other hand, if your magickal tradition has specific ways of blessing, charging, or consecrating items, you may want to work with those processes to honor your Path. As with any type of magickal methodology, go with what you know and trust for the greatest amount of success and personal satisfaction.

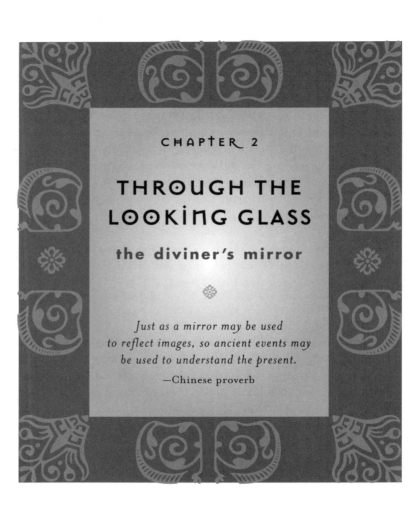

CHAPTER 2

THROUGH THE
LOOKING GLASS

the diviner's mirror

*Just as a mirror may be used
to reflect images, so ancient events may
be used to understand the present.*

—Chinese proverb

What does early Egypt have in common with Aztec temples and ancient China? All three of these locations and many, many others used mirrors as an entryway into other realities, especially for looking into the future. It's uncertain as to why mirrored surfaces got this reputation, but the best guess is that the reflection of a person's body on a surface was thought to be some type of soul or spirit capturing, similar to superstitions about photography.

SCRYING IN YOUR BEER?

While this book focuses on working with your magick mirror and other mirrored surfaces, it would be remiss to overlook the fact that scrying is not limited to this construct. Historically, those who practiced this art used a wide variety of media. Nostradamus, for example, often observed the flame of a candle to gain insights. The ancient Chinese stared at the sky and cloud formations so nature could unfold the patterns of the future. Other media for scrying included ink, wax, water, wine, coffee, soap bubbles, blood, and polished stone.

Not all seers used all media. Usually a person found one or two that worked consistently for her through trial and error (as will you). The beauty in this diversity, however, is the flexibility it offers. After you've learned the basic methodology, you can consider tinkering with alternative scrying surfaces if you're ever caught with a nagging question and are without your magick mirror.

HOW TO SCRY

A lot of people have never tried scrying, and many more have not been successful with the methods they've found. So before moving forward into how to interpret visions in your mirrored surface, I'd like to pause momentarily and talk about how to scry successfully. Before even going that far, however, please realize that the ideas presented here are not absolutely foolproof—they're simply what I've found works for a wide variety of personality types with about a month's worth of trial-and-error practicing. If these methods don't work for you, you do not have to follow this system to use the rest of this book effectively. In my opinion, use what works and don't fuss about the rest.

To begin, let's examine our terms. The word *scry* simply means "to discover." At its simplest, the art of scrying is that of gaining meaningful perceptions (visual imagery) from whatever medium you use for scrying, that is, a speculum. These perceptions are not discernable to others watching the speculum, and they may shift and change throughout the vision. Typically, these images don't fit with anything in your sphere of vision (environment), and, like dream interpretation, the symbolic value of the pictures can be very subjective.

In beginning your scrying efforts, it's best to realize that instant success is rare. This may take a little time and, more important, patience. Do not have any preconceived expectations and try to release yourself from that human fear of failure. Both will hinder how long it takes you to begin receiving images and the accuracy of the connected symbolism. Just as with any other art, this can't be coerced. In fact, tension is another huge deterrent.

The good news is that this process provides some users with amazing insights into self, others, circumstances, and even global matters. Since scrying is a type of autohypnosis, you are altering the normal functioning of your mind in defined ways. Akin to watching a movie screen, which provides a level of detachment, using the speculum provides mental space between the user and the past, present, and future. This space also allows us to examine even those painful places we all carry around inside us with a little less emotional connection.

Many people who have found other divinatory systems hard to learn or disappointing discover that scrying seems easier. Since the human mind tries to make order out of anything (even a blank surface), with scrying there's a tendency to have greater success in getting at least initial images. That's one of the reasons glitter or textures were discussed in chapter 1. That little something catches the eye, and in turn the mind tries to make a larger, whole image.

Also, since the predominant imagery in scrying comes from our own mind and spirit (versus our physical eyes), we have a gut-level understanding of potential meanings. It may take us time to comprehend that reaction and interpret it correctly, but it's there within us waiting to be tapped. In particular, parents who are bringing up their children magickally will find young people are quite adept at scrying. Their ability to imagine and visualize, let alone connect with other realms, is much higher than that of most adults. So much is this the case that many an ancient manuscript recommended youths for this work. For those of you thinking, "but I don't have children," don't fret. All those books and tapes on tapping your inner child will finally come in handy.

A third advantage to scrying is that it's a relatively low-risk type of divination. Since we have avoided calling a spirit into our mirror and have empowered it with an on-off switch, the images we receive will typically be coming from the Higher Self. The worst side effects, therefore, tend to be headaches from eyestrain, weariness, and sometimes a sense of imbalance or dizziness. Despite their level of concentration, most people find they remain fairly aware of their environment, which can also be a safety issue if they're burning candles or have kids.

The only time the images in your mirror may not be self-originating is if Spirit, a totem animal, a Guide, an Ancestor, or some other entity tries to use the speculum as a bridge. It's perfectly all right for the first four to be part of your mirror work, but just randomly chatting with disembodied souls that you don't know isn't the best idea. We'll talk more about this type of problem and solutions to it later in this chapter when we discuss problematic visions. Right now, however, this is a moot point since we haven't tackled an effective process for successful scrying yet.

THiRTEEN STEPS FOR SUCCESSFUL SCRYING

1. Prepare yourself. Make sure you're rested, healthy, and in a good state of mind before you begin. Being tired, sick, or angry puts you out of balance, and that negativity may not only result in really ugly imagery, but also possibly taint your magickal tool. Also, I recommend drinking a glass of water, avoiding overly heavy foods (like red meat), and taking time to do an auric cleansing in whatever manner is suited to your Path. Also consider the time of day during which you scry. Some adepts recommend waiting until night (not too late), because darkness speaks strongly of the intuitive self.

2. Clear the speculum. Even with an on-off command word and proper housing, your mirror may pick up some random energy between uses. So, give it a quick spiritual clean up using witch hazel tincture or just good old-fashioned soap and water. Note: Use this on the frame if washing the surface would harm your mirror's construction. Remember to focus on your intention.

3. Choose your working area and prepare it as well. Avoid areas with bad memories or those that make you tense. Tension, sadness, and fear become huge stumbling blocks to receiving psychic impressions.

4. Set the mirror in a spot easy to see, preferably at eye level compared to where you will be sitting. The larger the mirror, the farther from it you can be; however, most people find having it at reading distance makes for greater success.

5. Ensure your privacy and comfort. Turn off the phone, put up a DO NOT ENTER sign, or do whatever it takes to get ten minutes (or more) to yourself. (I've even gone so far as to lock myself in the bathroom.) Comfort is also important. Wherever you're going to sit, you'll want to be able to remain in that place without thinking about the ache in your back or your foot falling asleep. These things may happen at first just because you're trying to get your mind to focus on one thing instead of hundreds. Like a stubborn child being told "no," your mind finds other things to grab your attention. With time and practice, however, your body will stop distracting you, and slowly those itches, wiggles, and tweaks will cease.

6. Breathe and relax. Release any tensions and bring yourself to a state of alert ease, akin to when you're caught up in a really good book or movie. People who meditate typically do so at this juncture to help achieve this level of active spiritual awareness, opening their eyes when they feel ready to direct their focus toward the mirror.

7. Greet your tool. This is an especially important step if you've given your mirror an elementary spirit. To just start asking questions is rather rude. The indwelling personality deserves to be treated respectfully and with courtesy. Similarly, even without the elementary present, your mirror is a sacred implement. Honor that sacredness somehow in the mini-ritual that precedes its actual use. My method is to anoint it with the specially prepared oil that I spoke about in chapter 1. As I do, I also have time to adjust my inner energies so they more closely match the vibrations of the mirror. The more in tune you are with your tools, the less they'll produce static. Think of it this way: You're a clear channel (you've cleansed your aura and gotten your body, mind, and spirit focused on magick). Your speculum is a clear channel, having been likewise cleansed and prepared. Now you're making sure the lines of communication between you and the mirror are just as clear and sure.

8. Visualize light inside the mirror or just beyond it. This step is especially helpful if you find you're having trouble getting any results after thirty days of consistent effort. Sometimes all you need is a little bit of imagination to release your mind from mundane constructs. The only caution here is to be certain to differentiate between what you're willfully creating in your mind's eye and what is happening naturally. The best way for me to discern the difference is by having the imagined light appear in a specific pattern (like an upward white triangle). That way, if I see light of another shape or color in the speculum, this signals me that the actual process of viewing (and taking notes about what I see) has begun, and I can release the other image. You'll have to tinker with this yourself to see if the approach helps.

9. Express your purpose (verbally or mentally) and keep your goals clearly in mind. Most people come to the scrying session with a specific question. Whatever your purpose, it's necessary to communicate it to the mirror in some manner. Just as in *Snow White*, you may want to speak to

your mirror (words have power). If it helps, make up a little rhyme for yourself like:

10. Pace yourself. Start with small efforts—no more than ten minutes daily—and slowly increase. As with meditation, you're retraining your mind and spirit and exercising them in a new way to reach a receptive state to be able to draw out impressions from the subconscious and Higher Self. This can cause a bit of strain if you overdo it (your eyes may feel dry and weary or you might get a headache). I've found that using a timer, like one on a stovetop, helps me keep track of how long I've been at it. Every day or two, increase your goal by no more than two minutes (when you're practicing a new art those two minutes can seem to take forever). After four to six weeks, you should be comfortable with twenty-minute attempts. And after about three months, you can go far longer without being overly stressed—your endurance levels improve naturally just as with physical exercise. Just remain aware of your body. If it says "enough," listen.

11. When the experience ends, that is, input ceases to come forward, close or turn off your mirror in whatever manner you've decided. What's nice about this step is that it provides ritualistic closure for you too, not just the mirror. With repetition, you'll find that this closing process naturally begins to put your mind and body back into a normalized space and provide grounding.

12. Take notes. Do this as soon as possible while the images are fresh in your mind. If you're having trouble remembering a particular sequence, look back toward the mirror and see if that helps your recall. In this case, you won't be scrying, just giving your mind a mnemonic device.

13. Cleanse and put away the mirror. You might want to wash your hands before taking this step, as you're still carrying some of the energy from your session. If you can't wash, just flick your fingers to dispel any residuals into the Earth, and then take whatever measures you wish to purify the speculum and put it safely in its resting place.

Mirror, mirror help me see
How things truly ought to be
Let nothing be hidden, and clear images appear
While into your surface I now peer!

This particular chant would be good when you're trying to discover the truth about a person or a specific circumstance. In any case, whatever you do to keep yourself keyed to that overall theme helps fine-tune your results. As I mentioned before, other important missives will come through periodically, or you'll get a "can't answer now" response, but most often the firmer your focus and conviction, the clearer the visions.

And speaking of the body, I should mention that some people do not "see" things in the mirror; they smell, taste, hear, or feel something instead (or as an extra dimension to the vision). If this happens to you, you're not doing anything wrong. It's just your mind's way of communicating to you through a sense to which you respond in a metaphoric way. The hard part here will be learning to interpret the signals you get from your senses if there is no visual attached. To help with this, just consider your life's experiences, which you've been responding to through your senses since before birth. For example, a bad smell probably means "no" or a negative situation, whereas a fresh, pleasant aroma would mean "yes."

At the end of all this fuss, it's perfectly okay (and in fact healthy) to celebrate even the smallest amount of perceptual success. You saw a few flying sparks across the surface? Whoo hoo! Do the happy dance! Received a somewhat cloudy image that faded too fast? That's good news too! It's important to pat yourself on the back for those successes no matter how small or fleeting because this, in turn, builds confidence. The more you trust in your ability to scry, the more you're likely to see improvements in your future attempts.

SEEING IS BELIEVING

Much as, if looking into a burning mirror we see,
as with darkened vision, the great events.
—Nostradamus

Don't sit down at your first scrying session and expect to see a full-length movie with subtitles. Unless you have a knack for this art, that type of detail doesn't come until you've been working with your mirror for months (sometimes years). Don't be discouraged. Even small dots or light forms that appear can provide you with insights to questions, and typically that's what most people see within about a month of trying.

I suggest setting aside a little time every day for a month to practice with your mirror. Treat this time as you might a daily vitamin or other important part of your routine. Scrying takes time before most people achieve success, but, as I've mentioned, giving it four to six weeks usually yields results. If not, keep trying when time allows. It may be that, for some, scrying simply isn't the best form of divination through which to gain perspectives. However, that doesn't mean your mirror isn't still useful for the other activities mentioned in this book.

Besides making time to hone your art, consider some simple physical matters. For one, don't eat heavily before scrying. In particular, junk food, red meat, and rich sauces seem to consume a great deal of our physical energy that might otherwise be applied to the spiritual goal at hand. In fact, if you can eat several hours before scrying and give your stomach time to completely process and empty out waste, all the better. Also, wear comfortable clothing that won't distract you. Kick off those shoes and loosen up just enough to remain alert and not be cramped or uneasy.

The first time you think you see something in your mirror, you might hesitate or startle yourself out of the mental state and lose the image. Don't get frustrated; that's perfectly normal. Now you have a hint as to what to expect. Next time, just breathe through it and let the images come and go. Make mental notes of what you see so you can detail the experience later.

Each person's scrying experience differs, and each session can also create dramatically different visions. At one point an image will appear in a specific spot on the mirror; at another, you'll see only one image the whole session; and at another still, all kinds of images may dance on, or above and around, the surface, fading in and out. Sometimes you get sequences, sometimes nothing but a swirling mass of color that never forms. This, too, is perfectly normal—in fact, it's exactly the way your speculum should behave since each question, each purpose for scrying, is wholly unique to that moment.

The next obvious question is: how do you begin to understand what you're seeing and why? Hopefully, you've answered the whys when you greeted your mirror. Even so, there are times you will receive images about which you haven't asked or which seem to have no bearing on your purpose. This happens because a magickal tool is not simply keyed to you, but also to Spirit, and sometimes Spirit has something to say or something you need to pay attention to. So keep that in mind.

As to how to interpret your visions, we're going to explore some common imagery that appears in a mirror during scrying and interpret it based on fairly universal archetypes. Using a dream key sometimes helps. Other images, like geometric patterns, can be interpreted using a book of symbolism. However, I would always caution that your first impressions of meaning are typically far more important than any list of correspondences in any book. Just like your dreams, scrying imagery comes from the unconscious and the Higher Self. Thus, it's very subjective.

While archetypes give you a starting point for the images that turn out to be real head-scratchers, they are only that—a genesis from which you should continue digging deeper into the self to find the whole meaning. Also, don't try to make more out of an image than really exists. Literal images can often be interpreted without embellishment.

At first, the most common thing that scryers see are wisps of light or clouds. The brighter and clearer the light or clouds, the better the omen or more positive the answer to your question. Darker images tend to be warnings of some sort. Whatever your question, slow down and reconsider what you have seen. These simple images may grow more complex as you get better at your art. For example, a dark, cloudy form might be broken up by sparkling light, implying that while things may remain difficult for a while, there is still good reason for hope. Here are some other generalized interpretations for cloud or light-wisp imagery:

- ❀ **Movement up and to the right is a positive response.**
- ❀ **Down and to the left is negative.**
- ❀ **Clouds moving to where your strong hand lies are looking for greater clarification in the question.**
- ❀ **Circles without any real movement mean no answer is available right now.**
- ❀ **Bright red clouds often imply that anger or other intense emotions lie at the root of this situation.**
- ❀ **Orange wisps deal with harvesting from the seeds you've planted (the work of your hands or mind).**
- ❀ **Yellow clouds indicate the need to pay attention to the communications exchanged at that juncture or perhaps the need to be more creative in your methods.**
- ❀ **Green represents a growth opportunity.**
- ❀ **Blue clouds (especially sky blue) imply peace or happiness.**
- ❀ **Purple clouds talk of spiritual matters.**
- ❀ **Pink is a gentler form of red that usually deals with friendships.**

As time goes on and you practice more, it's likely you'll see far more than just clouds—also symbols and perhaps even three-dimensional images. As these detailed experiences become commonplace, you may suddenly realize you've totally lost sight of your mirror, having gotten caught up in the images. The first time this awareness hits you, it can be a little distracting, but try not to lose the pictures you're receiving, and don't try to bring the mirror back into focus. At that point, the gateway is already open within and without, making the tool simply a backdrop, so sit back and watch the show.

As images appear, pay attention to some specific things. When you're starting, it might be hard to remember these fine points, but with time and practice you'll begin to notice and recall them fairly easily.

- ❀ **The order in which the images appear**
- ❀ **Where images appear on the mirror in relation to other images**
- ❀ **Movement and its direction**
- ❀ **Reappearance of a symbol you've seen before in this sitting or a previous one**
- ❀ **Any overall patterns or sequences**
- ❀ **Split-screen effects**
- ❀ **How close or far away the image seems**
- ❀ **Other sensual cues that come forward during the sitting**

The order and placement of an image's appearance can indicate its importance, positive or negative influence, or perhaps a time line. Similarly, distances and movement could mean something in the past or future, something personal, or something less intimate.

Symbols that reappear, just as in dream work, are something you need to pay attention to, so don't ignore them. This is a nudge from your psyche. Patterns and sequences act like a connect-the-dots game. See what they tell you when you've gotten the full picture. Bear in mind that a sequence from one session may continue into another one if the question or situation is still unresolved.

A split-screen effect (where you see two distinct images or sequences played side by side) is a means of illustrating balance or imbalance or of providing comparisons. Other sensual cues provide depth and dimension to the experience. When you get these multilevel experiences, make sure to include all the potential symbolic value in your interpretation. Let's say, for example, you see the image of someone with whom you have business dealings smiling and looking pleasant. By itself, this might be seen as a good omen, but as this image develops fully you might start hearing static. To my thinking, the static is a warning that this person, while friendly enough, seems to have a hidden agenda or may be giving you false information.

INFLUENTIAL FACTORS

Say you've gotten little to no result from a mirror or the result you got was off somehow. What causes these kinds of things and how do you "fix" the problem? The first big help is realizing there may not be a problem at all. Perhaps the questions you've been asking of the mirror aren't well suited for its spiritual fingerprint. As the saying goes, ya can't get silk from a sow's ear (it makes you look silly and pisses off the pig). Similarly, you can't force a magickal item to function in a way that's opposite to or vastly different than its underlying matrix.

With this in mind, it's been shown that some specula reveal only specific things. One might work for relationship questions, another only for future visions, and still another only for personally pressing matters. This feature of scrying happens for a variety of reasons. It might be something the creator of the mirrored surface had in mind all along, or it might be a property of the object itself. Crystals in particular seem persnickety, more than likely because each one has unique facets and a makeup akin to snowflakes. So, be aware that if you're asking one question and you keep getting derailed toward another subject or theme, you may not be doing anything wrong whatsoever. In fact, you're responding to the speculum's individuality.

All things have a pattern, and you must respect the pattern of your tool. In this case, if the pattern eludes you, I suggest meditating with the mirror to get a feel for how best to use it. Or, try sleeping with it under your bed. In both instances, you may receive mental images that act as clues to the mirror's potential applications. For example, seeing a heart in a dream is a good indication that the mirror would work effectively for "questions of the heart."

A second thing that may influence odd or lacking results is your physical condition. Women in particular discover shifts in psychic awareness during their cycles, when pregnant, or when going through menopause. Some women's abilities skyrocket; others' seem to fade away or become skewed. Similarly, men may find their psychic aptitude increases or decreases with specific biorhythm cycles. This seems especially true during the late teens and again between forty and fifty years of age. While these variances are broad generalizations, they happen in enough people to make them worth mentioning.

Beyond personal physical cycles, eyesight has a lot to do with this art for obvious reasons. In particular, I've noticed something interesting among those who wear contacts and glasses. People often remove them for scrying in order to create a naturally blurry condition. On the other hand, your mind has grown accustomed to seeing better when you're wearing glasses. So, where one person needs to leave her glasses off because they remind her of mundane issues, another person might find keeping her contacts in place improves the results achieved. Again, the only way to know is to try both ways and see what's best for you.

A third factor in your outcomes (or lack thereof) can be timing. This ties into your body on one level and the Cosmos on another. Your body and mind are at their best during specific hours of the day. These "on" periods vary depending on your daily schedule, diet, physical conditions, and so on. For example, although I can hop out of bed and immediately tend to chores, I find my most productive hours are from around 10:30 A.M. until just after lunch (whenever that break comes). If you pay attention to your day, you'll find a similar time slot in which you know your senses are really keen. This is an excellent time for scrying.

On the cosmic level, the ancients believed that each day of the week, as well as various points in the day (and indeed, every hour), had planetary influences associated with it. Sunday, for example, is ruled by the sun, while Monday (moon's day) is dominated by the moon. Along these lines, you may find that specific types of questions are best asked at specific times. Dawn represents the future (a new day), while dusk deals with the past (endings). Noon symbolizes conscious matters, and midnight the subconscious or intuitive.

Fourth, consider potential external influences. I've found something as simple as rubbing my shoes over a rug can cause a speculum to malfunction because of the resulting charge I'm carrying. Similarly, static-filled clothing can cause problems, as can a room where someone recently had an argument or a region with vortexes and lay lines. Then, of course, there are more obvious things like a barking dog or honking horn.

Fifth, if the images are unfocused and lacking definition, perhaps your question was unclear and needs refining. The alternative possibility is that this is something about which you should not know yet or about which you're not ready to see the truth. In the case of the former, there are some things about the future that really cannot be known and others that could potentially harm us if we knew them. In the case of the latter, your mind simply will not let you see what it perceives as harmful to your psyche (that's why people repress memories).

Last of all, check your lighting. I don't like scrying with electrical lights blazing. I find they distract me. Candlelight seems far more welcoming and helpful. Nonetheless, the way light affects your results depends a lot on the colors you chose for the mirror, its framework and what might reflect off the edges, and your eyesight.

So, if you find you experience problems in one type of light, try a variety of others, including full-spectrum or colored light bulbs.

PROBLEMATIC REFLECTIONS

Sometimes the images you receive through your mirror might seem disturbing or make no sense whatsoever. When this happens, there can be a variety of reasons. One reason could be you were in a bad state of mind when you began the procedure. Anger, sadness, worry, doubt, and other similar conditions can project themselves into your scrying mirror as thought forms that you then see and interpret as ugly or frightening. When you realize this is the case, simply stop. Cleanse your mirror, put it away, and try another time when you're in better sorts.

A second possibility, especially for ugly or frightening images, is that your subconscious mind is projecting inner demons, like repressed memories or irrational fears. These are not necessarily images that should be banished back to the shadows. Psychologically speaking, there must be a good reason for them to come forward in this time and place. So what do you do with them?

For one, remember that the mirror gives you an external viewing screen and provides some emotional distance from such issues. For another, if you feel wholly unprepared, gather a few of the initial images into your memory and then put away the speculum temporarily. So that you have emotional support, find someone you trust to stay with you when you bring those images back up on the mirror's surface. In any case, when our minds decide to show us these dark places of the soul, it's best to examine them and bring them to light. A good motto for any magickal path is, Know thyself in truth.

The third reason for disturbing images is one we spoke of earlier, namely, the presence of a spirit with its own agenda. While this doesn't happen often, especially if you've placed a guardian elementary in your mirror, the speculum is a very real bridge between the worlds. You never know who exactly might be traversing that astral bridge when you get there, and sometimes those entities want to talk.

You have a lot of choices available to you at this point. The first is to turn off the speculum, cleanse it, and try again in an effort to reach a different "channel" or different location. However, some spirits are persistent and might still be waiting when you open the speculum again.

The second option is to listen to the spirit. If you choose this option in the hope that the spirit will say its piece and leave, I would issue one caution. Just because people are dead doesn't mean that they lose their humanness. Similarly, beings from other planes of existence have free will just as we do. Ghosts and other entities can lie and deceive, so take whatever message they impart with a huge grain of salt.

The third option is to tell the spirit to leave. Honestly, I don't like the idea of any being hijacking my scrying session unless it's for a good reason. This is your magickal tool, and no one has the right to use it without your permission. If the spirit doesn't heed your command to depart, do a small banishing spell or ritual. Usually, just starting one is enough to make the entity realize you're serious.

If nothing you do keeps an unwanted spirit away from your speculum, you may have to make a new one. Sometimes the construction of a magickal tool attracts beings with specific vibrations. They're drawn to it like a magnet. This is a rare occurrence but a possibility about which you should at least be aware.

A fourth and somewhat common cause of problematic images is random energy. While magickal practitioners try to learn to keep personal vibrations in check, there are many people in the world who are projectors. Whatever they're feeling or thinking goes out in all directions, hitting whatever people or things with which it comes in contact. Neither you nor your speculum will have immunity to this unless you've set up sacred space, which acts like a reflective bubble while you work.

There are many other causes for random energy signatures. Everything from memory imprints to psychic splashes can bring static into the connection you're creating. That static can distort and even completely reorder imagery. In this case, you can close the mirror and try again. Or, wait a while and then try again. Sadly, neither these problems nor their solutions work in a vacuum. They often combine, making your job a little more difficult, but having a clear connection is well worth the extra effort.

The fifth and very normal reason for odd images boils down to wishful thinking. We all have secret desires (and some not-so-secret ones). When we pose a question to our mirror, sometimes those background desires filter through. This is true for even an adept scryer. In other words, our hopes outweigh any imagery the Higher Self or Spirit may be trying to project because we're in the driver's seat.

More frustrating still, it's hard to distinguish these personal projections from actual divinations. That's where your scrying diary will come in handy (see the next section). Over time, you'll begin to notice the topics about which you got the answers you wanted versus the answers you needed. So when you pose similar questions in the future, take extra time to center yourself, release those personal desires, put down your ego momentarily, and in turn receive more accurate information.

LiTTLE BLACK BOOK

As with any metaphysical methodology, I highly recommend you start a scrying diary. Each time you use your mirror, make notes of the day, time, environmental conditions, and so on. Also note what images you received (if any) and what you feel they mean.

Return to this book and reread your entries every few weeks. Why? Lots of reasons. For one, you may discover that you remember more from your session as you reread it (add those notes in).

Second, reading over divinatory material after a little time has passed provides a different perspective. You may even discover that your interpretation of the vision changes or becomes clearer upon reexamination.

Third, a review of the material should begin to yield personal archetypes in the symbols you get from your speculum. As one specific image appears in different sessions, you'll begin to get a better feeling for its complete "personality," if you will. And while it may have more than one correspondence in your mind's eye, those relationships typically remain constant in any scrying effort. Your notes will clearly reveal these consistencies so you don't have to wrack your brain so much to understand the meaning behind your visions.

Fourth, and perhaps most important, your notes will show you in your own words the progress you've made. The first few efforts may have yielded little (or no) results. As you read on, however, you should begin to notice improved clarity, increased images, and more accurate interpretations. This immediately affects your overall confidence, which in turn improves the results you get in the future.

PAST, PRESENT, AND FUTURE VIEWING

The past remains with us like an echo that resonates on both the natural and the astral level. This soundscape is something with which your mirror can resonate. Why would you want to look to the past? Well, for one thing, to understand your here and now more completely. Your past brought you to this point, even the negatives. Your mirror gives you this great chance to step back and look at your life a little differently through the virtual viewing screen.

Think of it. You can watch your first steps as a child, see your first kiss again, come to grips with a painful memory, or find closure regarding an old argument. Everything in your life becomes an open book, unlocked by the magick mirror and your skills.

If you want to take this concept further, all history is available to you as well. Time is a human construct. In the astral plane, this construct doesn't really matter. There is no here, no there, no now or then—it works outside time. This means we can move along that plane and then use our mirrors to open specific windows.

Why would we want to do this? I can think of several excellent reasons. Suppose your family comes from a specific culture and that background is important to your traditions. What better way to understand those customs than to look at them through the eyes of those who lived when the tradition was just being born? I'm not saying this is easy. It takes a lot of practice to become that adept with your speculum, but it is possible.

Also, some people like to seek out past lives through their mirror. These lives remain in our soul like a distinct part of a fingerprint, and it's believed they can influence present behaviors and thoughts. So, uncovering them could prove quite revealing. The major difficulty in this specific search is releasing ego and preconceived notions. Not everyone can be Cleopatra or Plato, but it's normal for a person to wish that were true. As mentioned previously, your hopes and wishes can, and often do, find expression on the mirror as easily as a real past life memory. Please keep that in mind when approaching your mirror for this purpose and adjust your methods and perspectives accordingly.

Is there anything special you need to do to receive visions of the past? Not really. The key is your focus. However, there are some atmospheric touches that might help. For example, take a compact mirror, dab a bit of rosemary oil on it (rosemary is for remembrance), and focus on a question that has something to do with a past event. Breathe deeply and slowly, continuing to focus on your question. Allow your vision to naturally blur; you do not need to keep the mirror in complete focus for this process to work. At some point, you may see clouds or swirls appearing in the glass—or pictures, if you're lucky. Make a mental note of everything you see—the color, the direction of movement, and so on. When you've finished with your session, close the mirror, make notes, and then consider them in the context of the question you presented.

Next, we'll consider remote viewing of present circumstances—everything from marital issues to office politics, social concerns, and societal morals. Above and beyond getting perspectives on tough situations or choices, why else might one review the present?

Consider for a moment—life goes by at warp speed. Your day is filled with responsibilities, movement, and noise. How often during a day (or even a month) do you have time to sit quietly and integrate all that's happened and all you've learned? I'm willing to bet the amount is pretty minimal. Since you've already set aside time daily to practice scrying, why not make the most of that time, that is, do two things at once? In this case, when you get into a relaxed frame of mind, call up the day's images in the mirror and spend time processing all that's happened. Then take the best of it into yourself.

Another function of present seeing is checking on or communicating with someone you care about. Unlike the method we'll explore in chapter 3, this doesn't require that the other person have a matching mirror. However, I would suggest you gain permission from him to "peek in" now and again; otherwise, this strikes me as a tad intrusive.

To try this yourself, bring a picture of the person to the speculum earlier in the day. Leave it underneath or somewhere close by to begin attuning the mirror to his energy. When you're ready to begin, follow the steps previously provided, but rather than seeing a light in the mirror, you want to visualize that person. Just focus on the face. The rest may or may not materialize, but the facial expressions will give you an idea of his mental state. Once the person's image is clear, mentally reach out to him. Then, reach out with both your hands, putting one on each side of the mirror, and direct your thoughts through your palms. You can ask him later if he had any odd experiences while you were working. I realize this activity is only partially scrying, but it definitely ties into divination in that you're gathering information and communicating through paranormal means.

What about the big one that everyone seems to seek out—visions of the future? We're naturally curious about what tomorrow may bring. Will we be happy? Will we meet a lover soon? Will our jobs improve? The problem with future telling is that the future, unlike the past, is not a fixed state. So, how does any seer get accurate information about the future? The answer to that question is summed up in one word: habit.

Humans are, by nature, creatures of habit. Our daily routines follow specific patterns. Over time, those patterns become uniquely ours. When a seer reads cards or scrys, she looks for that pattern, and then simply follows a rather logical progression forward, like unrolling a long thread that begins at the querent and ends in a future moment.

Another theory of future telling claims that the visions we receive are actually a telepathic reception. In other words, the seer connects with a future someone through whose eyes she receives images. In this case, it's like being a television set and receiving signals that have already been created (since magick operates outside time).

No matter which theory you subscribe to, even one of your own devising, one thing is clear. Future images are iffy at best in terms of dependability, especially since our knowledge of the future changes our actions, which in turn can transform the future. And, in fact, that's one of the greatest rewards that comes from divination—the ability to take back the driver's seat with regard to our fate—as opposed to being hit head-on by it.

Is there any difference in the gathering methods for future insights as opposed to those for past or present? Not particularly but for the fact that your mind and spirit must reach forward, beyond this moment. Because of the significance of sacred space being "out of time," this is another occasion to consider creating a formal Circle (see chapter 4). Also consider visualizing the light in your mirror as appearing just beyond it, just as the future is beyond this moment. Remember, symbolism is important to the subconscious and the Higher Self.

Beyond that, you should be somewhat circumspect about the images you receive during future telling efforts. There's a danger of becoming so fixated on something that rather than avoiding it, you cause it. Also, don't make snap judgments based on the results. Keep your feet firmly planted in the here and now, and use what you learn to make careful, well-considered choices. In fact, this is good advice for any divinatory information.

ΑΠΥ ΠΟ-ΠΟS?

We've pretty much covered all the potential potholes we might run into during a scrying session but one, and that's becoming too dependent on the art. I know a lot of readers who tell me about clients who come again, and again, and again with the same questions. They not only go to that reader, but several readers repeatedly (I suspect in hopes of getting the answer they want, not necessarily the truth). These folks tend to fall into two categories. The first are spiritually hungry. They yearn for experience. The second group want to be spoon-fed the instruction manual for life rather than write it on their own. The first situation is one most of us eventually grow out of when we realize that real magick isn't flashy lights and fluffy bunnies. The second situation is more dangerous and potentially harmful to the individual.

Once you become adept at scrying, people may start coming to you asking for insights. It will be up to you to decide if you should, or should not, help. There are times when it's prudent to politely decline. The second situation I just described is one of them (otherwise you're enabling negative behaviors). The whole purpose behind divination is to access hidden or elusive things and then *apply* that knowledge. Most people in this rut avoid that second part. Nonetheless, without the second half of the equation, the sum is zero, zilch—basically wasted energy; you might as well dress up like a sideshow gypsy.

Other times you should decline include when you can't put aside any bad feelings toward the querent or when you already know too much about the situation involved in his question. The bad feelings tend to make for gloomy symbolism, and your knowledge can have a bearing on personal opinion quite unwittingly. Mirror readings should endeavor to be unbiased, honoring the truth aspect of the magick mirror, not simply ear-ticklers. Basically, if you keep the mottos of "harm none" and "do unto others" firmly in mind in your decision making and in your readings, you'll be doing very well.

BLiПDED BY ТHE LiGHТ

While I feel that nearly everyone using the approach in this chapter will achieve some level of success, there are individuals who have real mental barriers when it comes to visualization and image reception. And some may never overcome those issues, for whatever reason. The question for such people then becomes, how do I use my magick mirror? After all, you've taken the time and put forth the effort to make a wonderful spiritual tool. You don't want to just leave it lying around.

Do not despair. In chapter 3 you'll discover all manner of uses for your mirror for spells, charms, and other related activities that don't require the ability to "see." Also, there's nothing that says you can't get creative and combine your mirror with another divinatory tool such as a crystal pendulum. Quartz or moonstone pendulums in particular seem to harmonize with a mirror's energies. Just put your mirror flat down on a surface and your elbow nearby so that the point of the pendulum rests over the middle of the mirror. From this point forward, you can ask questions of the mirror (and pendulum) as you normally would and simply watch the pendulum's movements for answers. You will, however, want to have handy a list of movement correspondences. For this I recommend reading *Pendulum Magic for Beginners: Power to Achieve All Goals* by Richard Webster.

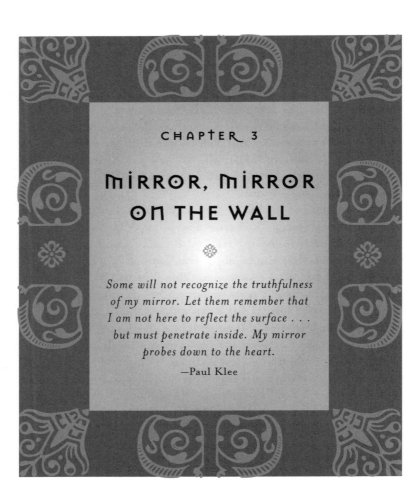

CHAPTER 3

MIRROR, MIRROR ON THE WALL

❧

Some will not recognize the truthfulness of my mirror. Let them remember that I am not here to reflect the surface . . . but must penetrate inside. My mirror probes down to the heart.

—Paul Klee

While it's common to think of magick mirrors only in connection with scrying (since that was a popular use), there are numerous historical accounts of other applications for reflective surfaces. For example, the Israelite women in Egypt used to flirt with their husbands using mirrors to entrance them and encourage fertility. Moses asked people to donate mirrors to the sanctuary, feeling them to be precious because the whole host of Israelites was born through them. The Bible also says that mirrors should be used to create washstands for priests.

Yet another illustration comes to us from Greece. There, an oracle serving Demeter (typically a priestess) would suspend a mirror over a sacred spring or well. Incense and prayers were offered; then the mirror was retrieved. At this point, the diviner looked into the mirror to determine if a sick person would recover or not. While this is certainly a type of scrying, it implies another function for mirrors, namely, a role in folk remedies.

The health-related application for reflective surfaces can be confirmed in a variety of texts, including those from India in which water blessed by the moon's reflection was given to patients to cure hysteria. This example beautifully illustrates how the ancients used the law of like curing like. Since the moon was thought to cause madness in some people, drinking of its reflection was a sure way to cure the illness.

With this history in mind, this chapter discusses using mirrored surfaces as a tool for reconnecting ourselves with our spiritual nature. In particular, we'll consider the role of mirrors in helping us empower our relationships, understand our dreams, overcome fears or obsessions, and improve self-images.

ETCHING OUT DEFINITIONS

Before sharing some spells, charms, and amulets with you, I'd like to take a brief moment for some groundwork. Experienced practitioners may not need this information, but please review it briefly anyway so you understand the terms as I'm using them contextually. And for other people who are newer to the craft, it's helpful to understand what's what before beginning any process. So, let's take a brief look at the differences in the basic techniques.

First, consider the word *spell.* Spellcraft is one of the keynotes of witchery. By definition, a spell consists of words set forth like a story in an effort to saturate an item with magick or release energy for a specific goal. Basically, it equates to a focused, willful prayer to which other components, such as movement or natural items, may be added to improve the overall sensual and spiritual experience.

Charms, amulets, and talismans are a little bit different from each other but certainly related. The problem is that these words have been used indiscriminately, one often being randomly substituted for the other. And while this might not be a huge issue (if the process works effectively), the reality is that charms, amulets, and talismans are three different constructs that suit different purposes.

Charms were likely the first form of spellcraft because they require nothing more than our words to invoke energy. The early charms were short verses often with a rhymed or lyrical quality (as implied by the root word for charm, which means "song"). This made charms easy to remember, and the practitioner didn't need to carry anything else to raise the magick.

It isn't until later in history that we see specific objects becoming the focus (or housing) for verbal charms. This is how the modern charm bracelet came into being—but with a lot more metaphysical focus, obviously. No matter what the form, however, most charms were designed to encourage love, improve luck, safeguard health, motivate prosperity or abundance, restore hope, and generally lift any heavy energy off the bearer's shoulders.

One thing that sets amulets apart from charms is their function. Traditionally, amulets were designed as preservatives, to safeguard the bearer from bad luck, defend his life or livelihood, and deter sickness. Another thing that differentiates the two is that amulets have always included one or more portable components as opposed to just words. The first amulets were made from bundled natural items like stones, bones, and plants. More fanciful amulets followed, etched in precious metals and sometimes designed with gems.

The amulet's power remains untapped until a specific situation calls it into action. So, if you have a travel amulet and you have a close call on the road, part of the amulet's power is used in that moment to protect you. Once that moment has passed, the amulet effectively turns "off" and waits until something else happens that requires its energy. This allows the amulet to last a fairly long time without having to be recharged, whereas charms are pretty much one-shot deals.

In contrast, a talisman is always "on," its energy surrounding the bearer constantly. So if someone works in a highly dangerous job, for example, having a protective talisman makes sense. However, that item will need regular recharging because its energy naturally drains off more quickly. Talismans were, at one time, created to house an indwelling spirit who would provide the energy desired. However, modern talismans are designed more like amulets during auspicious astrological phases and empowered using incanted charms.

SQUARING THE MIRROR

Now that we understand the definitions, the next thing to tackle is how you can go about changing a spell or charm or making one that's wholly your own creation. The metaphysical processes you come across in this and other books are what I call "shake and bake" magick. They're meant to be proofed and ready to go without requiring a lot of time in planning and preparation. However, some of them are not going to be applicable to your present needs and goals. In other cases, you may not have the suggested components handy or may find the pattern presented doesn't appeal to your overall spiritual vision. That's when it's time to pull out your inventiveness and do a little tweaking or consider designing something from scratch.

At this juncture, a lot of people get antsy, feeling that changing a spell or charm, or making one on their own, somehow goes beyond their experience level. If we bear in mind that many charms and spells are simple magicks and that someone, somewhere had to make the first spells or adapt them to broaden the usefulness of mystical processes, it becomes obvious that we're partaking in a venerable tradition. It's time to trust that voice within and reclaim your role as priest or priestess of your life.

The next question becomes, how? The answer to that depends on what you're attempting to do. If you're going to change a process you've found, what needs to change? Is it a wording issue? The lack of a component? Timing problems? Most of these are easy to solve. For example, the words of a charm should be words you can remember easily and are comfortable with. They need not rhyme, but many people find that rhymes make excellent mnemonic devices.

If, on the other hand, you're lacking a component, find a viable substitute. Consider the component's color, its magickal correspondences, its aroma, shape, size, and so forth. It's important that, no matter what the process, you maintain continuity of meaning and the items you end up using make sense to you. A good example here is the use of blood in many older spells. I'd probably use tomato juice or ketchup instead. The color here is right, and tomatoes have a connection with "heart issues" (the organ that pumps our blood). This substitution "squares off" effectively against the original.

If you like the overall construction of a process, but the focus isn't right for your goal, you'll need to change every part so that, rather like a puzzle, the whole fits together into an image of that goal. Your words, components, personal actions, and so forth become a blueprint to which the Universe can then respond via manifestation. Note, however, that if you leave out any part of the equation, or if you're not specific, your results may not be exactly what you anticipated. The Universe has a sense of checks and balances along with some pretty wicked humor. Sometimes what we think we need and what is really good for us are two different things, and how magick manifests often reflects those kinds of permutations.

And what of those times when you can find nothing you like? Well, draw up a blueprint from scratch. You can use everything you've learned from reading various charms and spells to determine how they go best together. But now you're stepping back for a moment and really thinking about your goal and how to best achieve it through words, components, and actions. This book is not the best place to discuss the entire process of self-created magicks, due to space constraints. Rather, if you would like to go further, consider getting some good books on spellcrafting, preferably those that include detailed component correspondence lists. In particular, my *Spinning Spells: Weaving Wonders* (Crossing Press) and *Magick Made Easy* (Harper Collins SF) may prove helpful.

MIRRORS FOR SPELLS, AMULETS, AND CHARMS

The wonderful thing about many spells, charms, amulets, and talismans is that you can take them on the road wherever you go. In our highly mobile society that's a huge asset. Speaking of which, let's get this show on the road and look at some sample mirror spells and charms.

Each of those that follow is named for the goal of the working so you can find what you need quickly. However, if something isn't listed here, consider looking for synonyms. For example, prosperity might equate to money in the entry.

Also, as we just reviewed, don't forget that you can adapt these or use them as prototypes in making personalized magick. If something works well for you as it is, then don't "fix" it—but if not, nothing here is carved into the mirror's frame. Better to change it than to waste time and energy on something that lacks meaning and therefore also lacks the power to manifest.

actualization amulet (confidence)

Many people are their own worst critics. They look into a mirror and see the wrinkle here, the blemish there—all the little imperfections. Nonetheless, those little things we wince about are also what make each person a truly unique individual. They reflect character and real-life experiences rather than a more plastic Barbie- and Ken-like facade, without feeling or depth. We may recognize that reality in our mind, but getting it into our heart is another issue.

I woke up one morning at the age of thirty-five and discovered I still suffered from teenage angst combined with a low self-image. Now, to my mind this was silly. I'm a happily married, professional woman and mother whose life is full. So what was going on beneath the surface here? The reality was that I carried around a lot of old wounds and outmoded ideas that desperately needed to be replaced with healing and a positive vision, and I know I'm not alone. In fact, a lack of self-worth often leaves people frozen in their tracks or, worse, wallowing in apathy. That is simply not the witchy way.

So, the purpose of this charm is stimulating a positive self-image, which in turn naturally opens the path toward confidence and actualization. For it, you'll need a compact mirror (easily portable) and a little bit of your favorite perfume or cologne, something that makes you feel really special whenever you use it. Prepare the charm around noon, when the light of conscious awareness is strongest, by taking it outside. Open the protective top of the compact and turn the mirror toward the sun to gather the light. Repeat this incantation four times, turning to each cardinal direction as you recite it:

Chase the shadows of the past
Outmoded outlooks cannot last
The light of truth and hope shall shine
In my heart and in my mind
And when upon this mirror I look

My spirit becomes an open book
Not to fear, but embrace
Negative self-images be erased!

Close the compact. Touch it lightly to your third eye (on your forehead between your eyebrows) and then to your heart. Keep this with you and look into it anytime you feel some of those old thoughts returning. Repeat the incantation, which you can tape on the inside of the lid if you have trouble remembering it. If you can't recite the charm out loud, don't worry—just think it. Thoughts are words uttered inwardly. When you've used the mirror four times, you'll need to recharge it in sunlight again.

banishing (overcoming)

What walls stand in the way of your personal or spiritual progress? What circumstances hold you back? What negatives do you wish to turn away so the Path of Beauty is filled with light and hope? The answers to those questions dramatically illustrate just a few potential applications for banishing amulets. With this in mind, I suggest finding several unframed mirrors of various sizes and shapes that you can prepare for different functions and have ready as needed. Then follow these steps:

1. Choose the shape of the mirror so it correlates to the area in your life where the energy of banishing or overcoming is most needed. For example, if you're having a long streak of financial problems, square is a good shape because this corresponds to Earth-oriented matters (foundations, prosperity, growth).

2. Find an aromatic oil that supports "turning" unwanted energies. Good options include bergamot, myrrh, vetivert, dragon's blood, clove, and mint.

3. Empower the mirror at midnight or at dawn when the power of light begins to overcome darkness. Alternatively, the waning stage of the moon supports banishing.

4. The process of charging the mirror is fairly simple. Visualize a vibrant white light filling it from the outer edges into the center until you can see it glowing within. Dab the center of the mirror with your chosen oil; then draw an outward-moving spiral (to move energy away), saying:

5. Put the mirror in the area where it will do the most good—if possible, in a window facing outward or some other place that's open to external influences so it can catch the negative energy before it reaches you. Keep any extra mirrors you've prepared in a dark, natural-cloth bag for future use. Before you put these out, repeat the incantation to reinforce the magick.

As night turns into day
All negativity, turn away, turn away
All that's evil, all that's bane

Cannot in the reflection remain
Return to the source, negativity flee
Liberate my home, my spirit—be free!

You can certainly change this incantation so it's more focused on your goal. You might also want to repeat it a symbolic number of times.

charisma charm

There are many moments in life where a little extra charisma could go a long way. For this charm, we're going to return to the example given at the beginning of the chapter about the Israelite women dancing to entrance. Sacred and magickal dancing is an old and powerful custom because it gives you the opportunity to literally put your energy into motion (and the motion itself builds the energy—it's truly symbiotic).

To make this charm, you'll need to work with your bathroom mirror since this is where we often primp and hone our outward image. If that mirror is too large to hold, you'll want to work in the bathroom facing it. If it's small enough, take it down and hold it in your arms as if embracing something precious.

Next, make sure nothing's underfoot and close your eyes. Think about yourself being attractive, with a strong, positive presence. Let that thought carry you into movement. Let your hips sway and swagger with confidence. Let the rest of your body follow.

Keep the vision of the charismatic you in mind while you dance. As you sense the energy reaching a pinnacle (you may feel warm, or your pace may increase), give the mirror an activating word that will release this energy when you recite it three times. Breathe the word onto the mirror's surface; then put the mirror back where it belongs.

The next time you feel the need for greater charisma, courage, or confidence, speak the activating word three times before you start using the mirror to shave or put on makeup. Close your eyes for a moment and see yourself again as you did in the dance. Accept the mirror's energy and then get ready to move mountains.

communication (talking mirrors)

The purpose behind this mirror is communicating with someone (or a group) over a distance. The most successful way to achieve this interaction is by making sure everyone involved has matching mirrors. These need not be the standard black scrying mirrors, but since part of the function of the speculum is that of a bridge in time and space, it's an excellent prototype. To that foundation I'd heartily suggest adding other symbolic touches that imply the mirror's function, like placing the mirror in a yellow frame (yellow is the color of communication) or painting the frame with the rune *Ansuz* (looks a bit like a capital *F*), which represents an awareness of messages and signals.

The communication effort should take place simultaneously, taking into account time zone differences. Wear similar clothing, burn the same incense, light the same color candles, and so forth. What you're doing here is creating sympathy between the individuals involved by following the same basic preparations (a mini-ritual of sorts).

Consider timing your effort for the waxing to full moon, which has better energy for opening the intuitive self. Sit before the mirror and bring to mind an image of the person(s) to whom the message is to be sent. Project that image into, past, or onto the surface of the mirror using your visualization skills. Once that image is clear, recite your message. Focus on it with your mind so that you're thinking out loud, directing the force of your mind and voice into the mirror and beyond it. Repeat the message several times—you may want to set a specific limit on how long you try to project the information, for both the sending and receiving ends of this conversation. When you're finished, close your mirror as described in chapter 2.

After making the attempt to reach out to your companion(s), take notes on what you saw or heard and compare them with each other by telephone or email. As with scrying, be aware that the message received may come through any one of your senses or even by an emotional expression (laughter or crying). For example, if someone were trying to tell you good news, you might find that you don't hear words or see images, but feel happy and hopeful.

I consider this particular activity to be among the more demanding in this book. Be patient and give yourself plenty of time to hone it—as Buddhists often say, the key to success is threefold: practice, practice, practice. Most people who stick with it, however, find this activity improves telepathic and empathic abilities.

dream catchers

Everyone dreams, even if they do not remember so doing. Dreaming is, in fact, vital to the human psyche. From a spiritual perspective, dreams have several other layers of importance. For one, if we can learn to create and interact with our dreams, that mental exercise can help us transform waking reality in positive ways. Consider for a moment that when you see something happen in a dream (even improbables like yourself flying), you tend to trust in it without question—that's a lot of faith-oriented energy that you can take into everyday life.

Another reason dreams are important is that they can become a vehicle through which Spirit can speak to us. Realistically, with most people's hectic schedules, this is one of the few times that the Higher Self or deity can get a word in edgewise over the clamoring conscious mind.

With dream interaction, you're basically bringing the conscious mind partially back "online" to transform the dream in ways that you'd like to see reality transform. With messages from Spirit or the Higher Self, you want to keep the conscious mind quiet and just listen. I've tried to blend these two goals in the design of this mirrored dream catcher.

To begin, you'll need a lace doily large enough to hold two two-to-three-inch mirrors in the center. You'll also need one round mirror (for the intuitive nature) and one square mirror (for the logical nature), along with silver-toned beads, gold-toned beads, moonstone beads, and quartz or fluorite beads. Adhere the square mirror to one side of the doily and the round mirror directly opposite the first on the other side. Around the square mirror, add the gold and quartz or fluorite beads in a square pattern. Around the round mirror, sew the moonstone and silver beads in a round pattern. This is really quite pretty when you're finished. By the way, you can knot wishes into the work simply by speaking a wish or an incantation into the knots you create to secure each bead. For example, on the lunar or round side say:

As above so below
Stitch and sew, stitch and sew
Bring to me Spirit-filled dreams
On the wings of moonlit beams.

And for the solar or square side say:

With each bead I stitch and bind
The key to waken my conscious mind
To interact with dreams by night
And manifest come morning's light.

Charge the square mirror in the light of the sun for four hours and the round mirror in the light of the moon for four hours. Finally, put the completed dream catcher on the wall over your bed. If that's not possible, you can put it on the ceiling or even on the floor beneath the bed, facing up toward your pillow. The visible side is what determines the energy you bring to your sleep time. So, on nights when you want to work on lucid and interactive dreaming, place the square side out. On nights when you want to receive psychic or spiritual dreams, place the round side out. Sweet dreams.

determination

When I ponder the attribute of determination, fond childhood memories come back of the little engine that could. So much of our success begins in the phrase "I think I can" (or perhaps even better—I trust I will). Determination in a spiritual sense is your will in motion, never being deterred. It implies constancy and a fixed purpose to which you apply energy until you've achieved your goal. Our determination spell begins with that fixed focus in mind.

For this activity you'll need a portable mirror. Any will do, but if you can match the shape to the specific area of your life in which you need more determination, it will improve the outcome of the spell. Why? Simply because every form of magick has a pattern as specific as a fingerprint. Love has a pattern. Prosperity has a pattern. Since you're filling your mirror with a specific pattern of power, it doesn't make sense to figuratively put a round peg in a square hole.

To help you choose your mirror's shape, remember that round and oval mirrors equate to the various attributes of the yin or feminine archetype, while square mirrors represent the yang or masculine. Yin-oriented goals include fertility, intuition, nurturing, steady growth, and the emotional or spiritual nature. Yang-oriented goals include leadership, rationality, authority, improved conscious awareness, and the physical nature.

Once you've chosen the mirror, the next step is to go somewhere private, preferably where you do the majority of your magickal work. Take with you a small image of the area of your life where you want to apply determined energy. Next, lay the mirror on a surface so you can see your reflection. Let that image saturate the mirror while saying:

What I see is part of me
What I say becomes the way
By my word and my will, all of vision be brightly filled
With but one goal, and with harmony of mind
In this mirror, my magick bind.

Now take the image you've brought with you and adhere it face down on the mirror's surface so the reflection of your eyes is looking at that image. Wrap this in a protective cloth and carry it with you into the situation where you want determination. Touch the mirror's surface like a touchstone when you feel your resolve waning.

employment

These days finding any job can prove difficult. Finding the right job is even more so. The purpose behind this charm is attracting the best possible work situation into your life. This might not be the ideal situation, but rather the best of the potentialities at hand.

The components for this activity are a magnet (if you can find one that illustrates the type of job you want, all the better), a portable mirror (larger than the magnet), your business card or area of expertise written on a piece of paper, and a success-oriented anointing oil like ginger or lemon balm. Attach the business card to the back of the mirror, with the magnet adhered on top of the card.

Now, dab the oil lightly on both the magnet and the mirror's edges while looking at the reflective surface. Focus intently on your goal while saying:

This mirror with its magnetic back
Holds within the power to attract
The work that's best, the job I need
By my will this spell is freed!

Remember to visualize yourself in the best possible job situation. Keep this token with you when you go on an interview. Touch it and mentally repeat the incantation just before you enter discussions or negotiations.

fear factor

Fear has positive functions, for example, instilling a sense of caution toward those things that could harm us. However, there are times when this emotion overwhelms us to the point of inaction. Spiritually speaking, some fears take on a life of their own as thought forms that attract more of what we most fear. And while working on one's perspectives helps, a little magick won't hurt in this situation either.

For this activity you can use a mirror of any size, but be certain it's inexpensive; a large piece of newspaper; and a black candle on which the word *fear* is carved. Take these to a place where you can sit undisturbed for at least fifteen minutes. Place the mirror on a table or other surface where you can clearly see it, and light the candle nearby. Now, turn your attention to the mirror as if you intend to scry, but think only about what you fear. Try to project an image of the fear onto the mirror. Once you've gotten a clear image, push that fear down into the mirror (if it helps, put your hands on top of the mirror and physically push as if moving something forcefully away from you), saying:

Into this mirror I willfully pour
All the fears that I abhor
Released from out my spirit and mind
The fears that constrain, in this mirror I bind.

Next, seal that fear inside the mirror by taking the black candle and letting it drip over the mirror. Remain focused until the word *fear* has melted completely off the candle. Then blow out the candle. Finally, wrap the paper around the mirror and put it on the floor. Crush it under your feet to destroy your fear and then dispose of the shards properly and walk away without looking back.

foundations (grounding)

In the words of Henry David Thoreau, "If you have built castles in the air, your work need not be lost. That is where they should be. Now put the foundations under them." When we're in school, our learning requires strong foundations. Spirituality, if it's to remain firm, requires strong foundations too, and that's just naming two of life's many situations in which having a sturdy substructure is not only handy, it's vital. When you find you're having trouble creating that foundation on your own, try this spell.

Gather the following components: a small mirror, seeds from a flowering plant, a plant pot with potting soil, and a small biodegradable image of the area in your life that needs improved foundations. Wait until the waxing to full moon for growth-oriented energy; then empower the mirror by looking in it and saying:

Hope within this image shine
Put down my roots, in my branches intertwine
No winds shall blow, no fires burn
That n'er will my foundations upturn.

Place the mirror deep in the soil facing upward. Next, take the image you've chosen and hold it between your hands. Visualize your need in every detail possible and then put that image into the soil just above the mirror. Next, take the seed and name it after your need. Bless it, saying:

This seed I sow
Foundations to grow
As above, so below!

The seed then goes into the pot just above the mirror and the image. This way, as it grows, the roots wrap around both, providing support. Tend this seed with loving care. By the time it flowers, you should see substantial improvements in stability.

glamoury (illusion)

It's believed that witches learned the art of astral illusion from the fairy folk, who loved to play tricks on unsuspecting humans. What exactly is glamoury? It's the art of putting into your aura a pattern (energy) that subtly shifts other people's perspectives toward you. This isn't like shapeshifting, but more like wrapping yourself in a cloak that lets people see only what you most want them to see.

While I don't recommend maintaining glamoury with family and friends (since you want to be wholly real with such people), there are times when this ability comes in quite handy. For example, it's useful for meetings in which you want to exude an air of complete control and confidence (even though your stomach has vultures flying around) or when you want to put your best foot forward on a first date and really shine with inner attractiveness. In both situations, you're not creating something that doesn't exist somewhere in your being, but rather bringing the positive to the forefront. Here's how.

Get a handheld mirror. You can prepare it like a scrying mirror if you wish, as long as you keep the end use in mind in your preparations. You'll also want to make a tincture for blessing this mirror that uses plants like heather, vetivert, clover, hawthorn, rosemary, and thyme, all of which have associations with transformation and appeasing fairy folk. Make this when the moon is fullest at midnight (the witching hour), if possible.

To prepare the mirror for glamoury, apply the tincture to the surface while you stare into it and visualize or project the kind of bearing you wish to create. Wipe the tincture onto the surface, starting at the outer edge and moving inward slowly as you say:

Mirror, mirror let all see
What's truly inside, what I can be
From my heart to my aura _____ *draw out*
And then perceived by those about
Mirror, mirror, let all see
By my will so mote it be!

Fill in the blank with the theme of your goal, such as confidence, bearing, or courage. Continue to chant as you look in the mirror until a complete image forms and you feel a real connection to it. When you're finished, return to the mirror and clean off the tincture, wiping it counterclockwise to release the glamoury.

insight (perspective)

We've spoken to some degree of how the scrying mirror can provide us with alternative perspectives into situations or individuals. This surface was designed to be honest with us and reveal what we cannot normally see. In this case, you'll make an amulet that protects you against false perceptions. You'll want a small portable mirror about the size of your palm. You'll also need a piece of white or silver cloth two-and-a-half times the size of the mirror, rose and marigold petals, and a bay leaf.

Wait for the three nights of the full moon to charge your mirror. On the first night, write the word *insight* on the bay leaf (this is based on an ancient form of wishcraft). Next, burn the leaf in a fireproof container. As the smoke rises upward, say:

Hear my wish upon this night
Grant to me the gift of insight!

Let the bay leaf burn out naturally while you continue to focus on your goal. Set aside the ashes for the following two nights. On the second night, lay your mirror out under the moon (somewhere you can leave it for the entire night). Blend together the ashes and the flower petals and sprinkle them around the mirror, saying:

> *Psychic site in rose and marigold*
> *Let my eyes the truth behold!*
> *When I look upon this silver glass*
> *Grant perspective and hold it fast!*

Leave the mirror and the herbs where they lay. On night three, gather the mirror and whatever is left of the herbs into the white or silver cloth and bundle it with a string. Carry this sachet with you. When you're not pressed for time, look to the mirror to improve your insight into a situation. When you need perspective quickly, release a pinch of the herbs to the wind with either incantation. When the herbs are gone, you'll need to recharge the mirror.

luck

Everyone can use a little extra good luck, especially when you feel as if you're having a streak of bad. While in part we make our own luck through our attitudes and actions, a little magick can get the energy patterns of our life moving in the right direction again when they're askew. This charm is designed so you can use it to help turn the tide in your favor.

To make it, you'll need two mirrors of the same size and shape. If you can find some that have a personally lucky number of sides, all the better. Sometimes you can have a glass cutter make them for you. You may wish to create this charm on a Sunday at noon. According to lore, this time of day and this day of the week are both propitious for inspiring more blessings, and luck is definitely a blessing. Put both mirrors in the light of the sun, saying:

Spirits of bad luck chased away
By the powers of light, by the shining day!
And when these mirrors twist and turn
All good fortune shall return!

Glue the two mirrors back to back. Next, take a piece of sturdy cord or ribbon and adhere it to the edges of the two mirrors so you have a loop from which to hang them. Put this on a wall near your altar and when you need a change of fate, turn the mirror and repeat the incantation.

memory mirror

Is there something you don't want to forget? Is there a special person or an event you'd like to remember in its entirety? Then this is a great little magickal token. For it you'll need a mirror with a magnet on the back. You can buy one at a store that carries refrigerator magnets, or make one by gluing a smoothed piece of aluminum foil to a mirror that is light enough to stay in place when you hang it up. You'll also need some rosemary oil and a piece of paper on which the topic to be remembered is written—it should be small enough to adhere to the surface of the mirror without covering the whole reflective area.

Since memory is connected with our conscious mind, work during daylight hours particularly on a Sunday (the sun's day), since solar energy supports your goal. Place the note (or symbol) on the reflective surface you've chosen, saying:

> *The light before me lights the way*
> *Whenever I see this, my memory sway*
> *Certain to know, my magick here bind*
> *_____ recall to my conscious mind!*

Fill in the blank with the focus of your remembrance spell. Now, here's the important part. You need to put this where you can see it regularly—the refrigerator is ideal. Every time you pass the reflective surface, bring the incantation into your thoughts, and thereby also what you need to remember.

money

Money may not buy happiness, but it sure makes being content a little bit easier. Also, not worrying all the time over the bills gives us a little more energy that we can then apply to our magick and spiritual pursuits. With this in mind, you can make this money charm with a small swatch of green or gold fabric and a tiny mirror like those used for fabric decoration—you can buy them in most fabric and craft shops for under $2.00. A square reflective surface is best for this since it supports strong financial foundations. You want the finished charm to be small enough to carry in your purse or wallet.

In terms of timing, you might want to make this on a Wednesday for resourcefulness or on a Monday to encourage both creativity and abundance with your finances. Look into the surface of your chosen token and speak into it your need. Know that you're whispering across the planes, extending your wishes to the four winds and the Universe. Repeat your need four times; then wrap the token in the gold or green cloth. Bless it using the following incantation repeated four times:

I place this with my money stash
To bring a steady flow of cash
Not for wealth, or for greed
But to bring me what I need.

Put this in your purse or wallet, preferably with your bills. You'll need to recharge the charm after you've received four unexpected influxes of cash, such as finding a forgotten bill in your pocket, having a winning lottery ticket, or getting an unexpected refund.

travel amulet

I do a lot of traveling by car and airplane and know full well the dangers that exist out on the road. Our society is very mobile, and there are dangers that we can't anticipate or wholly avoid. The purpose of a travel amulet is to create a buffer of protective energy you can carry with you.

I've made two of these amulets—one to hang from the rearview mirror of my car. You can simply bless the rearview mirror if you wish, but I like having a separate item that I can remove and recharge as needed. Begin with a circular mirror. The circle represents boundaries and safety. You'll also need four pieces of elementally colored felt—red, green, yellow, and blue. Cut four equal-sized squares of the felt and stitch them together. Recite this little chant as you work:

> *Earth and Air, Fire and Sea*
> *Protect my travels*
> *Blessed be!*

If you don't want your stitching to show, you can make another large square the same way and glue the two squares together, finished side out.

Next, using fabric glue, attach the mirror to the center of the squares. If you plan to hang the amulet from your car's mirror, you will probably want to stitch lightly over it two times for strength

You can use a single strand of heavy thread and crisscross over the surface of the mirror to create a pentagram. While you're securing this in place, you can add an incantation like:

> *A shield of protection abounds*
> *An air of safety surrounds*
> *Reflect all dangers, safe I shall stay*
> *Whether I travel by night or day.*

Now hang this in your car or put it safely in your carry-on luggage. If you feel danger approaching, touch the amulet and mentally or verbally recite either of the verbal components.

By the way, the basic process for making this amulet can also be used to protect your health. Change the first chant so it reads:

> *Earth and Sea, Fire and Air*
> *I put my health in your protective care!*

Change the second incantation so it reads something like:

> *A shield of health abounds*
> *Elements of well-being surround*
> *Healthy in body, healthy in mind*
> *In this charm, fitness I bind!*

truth talisman

How does one determine the truth of any words or situation? There are times when we feel in our guts that something is awry, but we often brush off those instincts. Rather than always second-guessing our intuitive nature and blaming indigestion, why not make a truth talisman that will encourage an improved sense of true seeing?

In ancient times, the ability to see true not only touched on determining the truth of situations, but also aided in finding thieves, predicting the future, and so on. So, you can put a lot of different energies into this talisman to aid you with a variety of goals if you wish.

To make this, you'll want a mirror (you choose the size, and it can be prepared for scrying if you wish) and a quartz crystal for clarity. You'll also need good quality craft glue or some silver wire to attach the quartz to the center of the mirror's surface. Once you have attached these two items, leave the mirror and stone to charge in full sunlight for four hours and in moonlight for five hours—discerning truth involves both the conscious and intuitive selves. Empower the token, saying:

In the center of my reflection—clarity
In the center of my reflection—truth
All instincts substantiated by proof!

Let nothing be hidden, realities reveal
Nothing amiss can be concealed!

Carry this with you into any discussions or situations where you feel something may be hidden from you. If possible, keep one hand in physical contact with the crystal (the center of the reflection) while you talk, listen, or interact. Pay particular attention to the details you're receiving as well as how your Higher Self responds to those details.

promise me mirror

Promises may be easy to make, but not so easy to keep. The purpose behind this spell is supporting one's sincere desire to keep a promise to another or to a group. To begin, you'll need one mirror per person, glass paints in personally pleasing colors, and a tray covered with rich potting soil. You need enough surface in the tray so that those who have brought mirrors can place them into the dirt together. This particular part of the spell comes from an old European custom of having the Earth witness an oath (since it will be around to watch the outcome far longer than we).

At the outset, each person needs to mark her personal mirror with her name or an emblem to represent herself. Use glass paint for longevity. Put the mark in the middle of the mirror while you look into it speaking of your promise. Look yourself in the eyes and make sure you mean it. After the paint dries, everyone puts the mirrors into the soil. Bless them in unison, saying:

Soils of the Mother, hear our pledge
With these words and tokens we promise _____
Bless these mirrors to remind us of our sincerity
And to motivate perfect action toward manifestation
So be it!

At this point, you can exchange tokens (thereby carrying the other person's word of honor with you) and take the soil outside. Scatter it to the four winds together, knowing that the elements and guardians now hold your promise.

psychic safety

If you believe a person is sending negative energy your way, write his name on a small mirror that you can wrap easily in white cloth. White represents protection, and since you're wrapping the name inside on the mirror, whatever the person sends out will be directed immediately back. This is a particularly nice amulet in that it activates only if that person intends harm. In other words, you can't accidentally send negative energy to an innocent, which makes really bad karma.

By the way, if you have a picture of the person, you can put it face down on the mirror and glue it in place. This creates a specific reflective energy that will help the individual see himself in truthfulness.

* * *

This is a small sampling of the kinds of amulets, charms, and spells that you can create with your scrying mirror, plane mirrors, or other reflective surfaces. Don't forget to let spontaneity and Spirit guide you in finding and using many, many more.

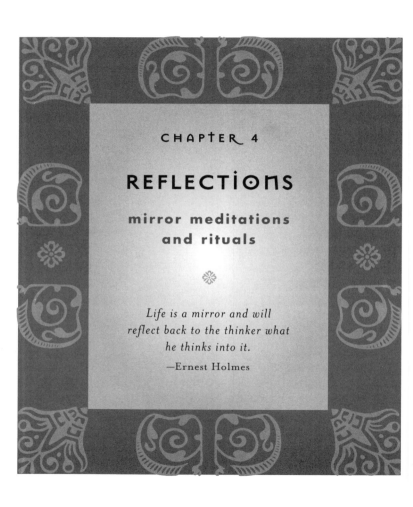

CHAPTER 4

REFLECTIONS

mirror meditations
and rituals

❖

*Life is a mirror and will
reflect back to the thinker what
he thinks into it.*

—Ernest Holmes

Building on what you've learned about spells and charms in chapter 3, we'll move forward to using mirrors as meditation and ritual tools. Specifically, we'll examine placing mirrors in the ritual space to welcome protective powers or as ritual components and meditations that employ mirrors as a starting or a focal point as a part of visualizations. These two applications work nicely together since witches and pagans often use meditation to prepare for ritual and many rituals often include meditation as a component.

MEDITATIONS

The basic definition of the word *meditate* is to think deeply, review-ing something in your mind while your body remains at rest, but this really only skims the surface of the ways in which people have practiced meditation over the years. Taoists, for example, seek an inner silence. Other people use meditation as a means of com-muning with spirits and as a bridge to astral journeys, which makes this technique a perfect aid when working with a tool that's already an astral bridge, namely, your mirror. Magickal practitioners use meditation for all the above-mentioned goals, depending on the needs of the individual at the time. We also know from modern studies that meditation has numerous benefits, including lowering blood pressure, improving concentration, inspiring an overall peace, and even increasing productivity in the workplace.

Meditation is an ancient art. The first time someone got lost in thought he was meditating. So it may well be that the ability to meditate was discovered in one of the most traditional ways possible—by accident. Consider the tribal drummer sitting and pounding out a rhythm who suddenly realizes that hours have passed since she began. This person did not do anything different; something just happened. Meditation is something completely natural to our species.

Natural things aren't necessarily easy. Meditation asks your body to stop moving and your mind to narrow its focus away from the hundreds of things it normally does every moment toward one thing or nothing at all. As we briefly review helps and hints for successful meditation, my first word of advice is to be patient with yourself. Don't set unrealistic goals or anticipate lofty results. Rather, set aside a specific amount of time for practice each day and your ability to meditate should improve slowly and steadily. This can be as difficult to learn as scrying for some, but the time and effort will eventually pay off.

keys to successful meditation

Can you sit, stand, dance, or even drum when you meditate? Yes! I often type when I meditate (it's amazing how much gets accomplished during that time). In Eastern mysticism, it's said that anything can become a kind of meditation; the only differences are your attitude and level of concentration. Returning to my example of typing, if I take a deep breath, really relax, and make sure things around the house are quiet, suddenly ten pages have been completed without my realizing it. Meditation allows the words and ideas that sometimes get stuck in mundane mud to simply flow without so much struggle or "head work"—which in spiritual writing seems to be a good thing.

If you're just starting to meditate, you'll want to try the basics recommended here in various physical positions—sitting, standing, lying down—or during various types of movement like walking, jogging, or biking. Wear comfortable clothing, be well rested, and ensure yourself of some uninterrupted time. Start out slowly in, say, five- or ten-minute attempts and increase the amount of time as you become more proficient.

Experts tell us that immediately upon waking or right before a main meal are the best times to meditate, but you should choose one time that can remain consistent. They also claim that adding incense or aromatic oils, chanting or mantras, drumming, candlelight, visualization (purposeful daydreaming), and other sensual cues can help improve the overall experience. If you must eat before you meditate, avoid heavy food and consider eating something associated with the moon (which correlates with our intuitive, spiritual nature). Included in this list we find milk, egg white, barley, fish, poultry, yogurt, rice, and cauliflower.

You'll have to experiment with the best combination of components for you. I strongly recommend keeping a notebook of your attempts with the following details:

- ❀ **Time and date**
- ❀ **Location and environmental conditions**
- ❀ **Purpose**
- ❀ **Length of attempt**
- ❀ **Sensual components**
- ❀ **Impressions gathered**
- ❀ **Notes on the overall experience**

Refer to this meditation diary later. By doing so after several attempts, a pattern of successful elements should begin to emerge. Once you know what elements help you the most, use them regularly—akin to a mini-ritual that will help transport your mind and spirit into the right framework.

Remember two words: *breathe* and *be*. Breathing is one of the most universal and central parts of meditation. Begin by taking a deep breath in through your nose and out through your mouth. Fill your lungs from the bottom up. Repeat this several times until the end of one breath naturally cycles into the beginning of the next (you're making an unending circle of air).

Now close your eyes. Continue breathing and simply let yourself be. Hear your breath. Hear your heart beat. Listen to the sounds that are wholly you. Do not be surprised if you find parts of your body distracting you—an elbow might itch or your nose feel a tickle. Try to ignore that and continue working through the discomfort with the breathing. With diligence you can get past that stumbling block, and it's a perfectly normal part of retraining your mind and body for such purposeful focus.

Turn your mind wholly to the task at hand—the reason for your meditation. Remain aware of sensations and impressions that you get. When you feel you've gone as far as you can for today, let your breathing return to normal and open your eyes slowly. Put your hands on the floor or ground and make sure you're wholly in yourself. Stretch a bit before getting up, and don't move too quickly as it can cause a headache.

Your meditative successes will naturally vary with your environment, level of focus, and personality. Nonetheless, even a little quiet time breathing and relaxing is beneficial. As you reach deeper levels of meditation, you may find yourself feeling tingly— as if the body doesn't exist. Some say this is the state in which you can learn to astral travel if you wish. This is also the time when you can commune with helpful spirits, animal totems, and your own Higher Self. Do a lot of listening.

visualization

All the meditations in this chapter include some type of visualization. You know the old saying, "seeing is believing." The power to change our reality begins with our thoughts and our senses. Visualization allows us to create an image of something we seek, experience it remotely, and then bring that "belief" into our waking reality.

As with meditation, this can prove difficult for some people to learn. However, if you've already worked through the scrying chapter of this book, you'll find that a lot you learned there applies here too. And if you ever enjoyed any "hunt for the hidden pictures" games or daydreamed as a child, that experience can also prove quite helpful.

Visualization hands us the keys to our thoughts by refining and guiding their energy. And while you might think of visualizations as only visual, they can have audio, tactile, aromatic, and taste dimensions if you respond to those senses more strongly. The only difference is instead of, or in addition to, calling up a portrait of your goal, you're now going to call up an associated scent, sound, taste, or touch.

When you start trying to visualize, don't reach for complex imagery. Begin in black and white, like a simple geometric (I find white imagery on a black backdrop is easiest for me). Once you become good at seeing those kinds of images in your mind's eye, make them slightly more and more complex. Eventually, you can add color, dimensions, and even whole outtakes from your day. If you think of this as watching a movie provided by your imagination, that also sometimes helps the clarity of results.

the meditations

There is a wide variety of meditations to which your mirror might make a useful addition. I provide several examples here for you to try or adapt. Since it's hard to concentrate on your experience and read at the same time, you may want to memorize these or tape them. If you are tape recording, make sure to speak slowly and put in pauses that give you time to bring up the imagery and make various shifts in your awareness.

TRAVELING THE WORLD TREE

A metaphorical depiction of the spirit world as a tree occurs in Cabalism and shamanism. We're going to adapt the symbolism into a meditation that helps you move between realities using your mirror as part of the visualization process. Learning to do this will help you in many ways, from being able to commune with elemental spirits to opening your Higher Self to ongoing communication with the divine.

Set up your scrying mirror in front of you on a table and sit in a comfortable, straight-backed chair. Stretch a little, shake out any tension, and begin breathing slowly and evenly. In your mind's eye, bring up the image of a huge oak tree whose trunk bears a doorway and project that image onto your mirror or just past it, depending on what's most comfortable for you. When you have that image clarified, open your mirror in whatever way you have designed (see chapter 1). It helps if you combine this with a pantomime of opening the doorway in the tree trunk using your strong hand (the one you write with).

Let your spirit move into the visualization in front of the tree's door. You'll notice there's a set of stairs heading downward. That's where you'll begin. These are the roots of the tree, and they reach throughout the Earth, feeding it. Your feet can become part of those roots, as strong and sure, as wholesome and nourishing. This is the part of the tree where, if you wish, you can meet with people in your life who have passed over. It is also the place where you can deal with past life issues and anything that's outmoded in your life. Give it to the Earth's soil. She knows how to handle our dirt.

Your legs will begin to stretch out from those roots, moving your body, arms, and head up toward the middle realm. This is the natural world as it is today. This is a place where you might meet animal guides, totems, and devic spirits and gain their assistance on pressing matters. It's also the region in which to meditate on pressing matters in your everyday life. Don't be surprised if you see your mirror sitting somewhere in this realm. It's your doorway back to the here and now, and it's also something into which you can look to discern the truth of a matter. Linger here for a while, see what images appear, and listen carefully for any messages that nature may have for you.

Now your legs are growing again, becoming large trunks to bear you upward toward the sky. This takes you outward to the stars, where you can discern your place as a citizen of the Universe, commune with the deity, ponder your hopes and dreams for the future, and also speak with the Ancestors or Ascended Ones. This is perhaps the loveliest spot in the world tree (for me anyway). I like to linger here and feel the oneness with all time and space, listening to the rhythm of the Cosmos. And as you look to that sky with all the small dots of light and life, it is your mirror yet again, reflecting back to you all the potentials of today, tomorrow, and forever.

When you feel ready to leave, slowly pull yourself into your roots. You'll notice how connected you feel to the Earth during this reversal process. This will also help you ground and center. When your mental image returns to that of a normal person, return out of the doorway you entered. Bring your spirit back through the mirror into your body and breathe evenly. Take notes of your experience afterward.

TOTEMS AND ANIMAL HELPERS

We've discussed the role of mirrors as bridges between realities. In this case, you'll be using that bridge to reach out and find your animal totems and helpers. Before moving into the meditation, however, I'd like to take a moment to clarify the difference between totems, power animals, and animal guides.

A totem is the spiritual form of a natural creature that becomes a lifelong spiritual partner. A totem may be personal or attached to a group, such as a Native American tribe with Bear as a totem. This being contains all the attributes associated with the natural animal and its metaphysical energies; thus it may be called upon in astral journeying to protect and guide, provide insights into a situation, or share its attributes with the practitioner as needed.

Power animals are similar except that they may not remain with a practitioner throughout his life, but rather come as circumstance dictates. Power animals can work in tandem with other creatures in the astral realm, whether or not they're connected in any way with the practitioner.

Animal guides are what you might expect, beings that come with a lesson or a specific message for the practitioner. These typically do not remain past the time when their presence is needed. I mention this because it's easy to mistake one for the other and then suddenly realize an animal friend is gone. Rather than wonder if you've done something wrong, you can recognize that it was a power animal or animal guide rather than a totem.

For this meditation, it helps to be somewhere out in nature, but if you cannot be, the visualization creates a surrounding that will welcome various animal forms. Begin as you did with the world tree visualization, sitting comfortably in front of your mirror. This time, however, create the image of four distinct landscapes in your mind with yourself in the center—somewhat like being the center of a living mandala.

To the east of you, see a cliff, high and untamed. Feel the gentle winds that roll from that direction. (If it helps, you can set up a fan to the east of where you're meditating to improve the sensual cues.) To the south see a desert. There's a dry, rich heat emanating from this area. (You could place a floor heater behind you.) To the west is an oceanfront, with gentle waves that roll in and kiss your feet. (If you have a water fountain or a nature CD with the sounds of water, put that to the west of where you sit.) Finally, in the north lies a lush forested region. (Some woodsy incense might help with this part of the visualization.)

When you clearly see this image in your mind's eye, project it onto or beyond your scrying mirror and open the mirror in whatever manner you've designed. Bend close to your mirror and whisper these words across the realities:

Of Earth, of Air, of Fire, of Sea
My power animals come to me!
And as the across the realms I sing
Into this space, my totem bring!

Continue chanting these words for several minutes until your voice naturally quiets; then wait and watch the surface of your mirror for images. Give yourself at least fifteen minutes of observation time. If you see any animal figures, pay particular attention to where the image originates. Images in the center of the mirror are more likely to be totems, whereas those appearing in any of the four quarters are more likely to be power animals. If you don't see any images, you can repeat this meditation at another time and reach out again. Spirits will not always be available to answer us.

When you're finished, move your mind back out of the mirror's space and begin to readjust your senses. Make notes of your experience in your journal.

If animal spirits were kind enough to come to you, do some research on their powers and meanings afterward. It's also important to honor those beings as helpmates in your spiritual growth—some people get a tattoo of the animal, while others keep carved images on their altars. If you neglect your animals, they may leave you.

GOD/DESS WITHIN

The phrase *Thou art God* or *Thou art Goddess* often appears at the end of neopagan letters as a farewell that honors the divine within each person. Nonetheless, I hazard to guess there are many days when each of us feels far less than divine. Yet even when Spirit seems far away, it's good to remind ourselves that god/dess hasn't gone anywhere. It is only our perception that's wanting. Thus, the purpose behind this activity is to reconnect with that inner divine spark using our mirror as an open, soulful window.

You can use any size or shape of mirror for this activity, including your scrying mirror. Set it on a table before you and begin looking into or past it as you would to begin a scrying session. Bring up your own image, however, exactly as you sit right now. Slowly narrow that image to focus on the area of your heart chakra. Whisper gently into the mirror:

Open the way, open my heart,
To see the god/dess within,
To touch the divine spark.

Keep repeating this evenly as you continue to watch the mirror's surface. After a few minutes, you should begin to see just over your heart a swirling of light that opens like an iris. Inside is a flame of the purest white-blue light imaginable. Focus your attention on that flame. Let it grow in the speculum until that is all you see.

As you watch, let your own image develop out of that flame—pure, glorious, powerful. Reach out to embrace that image—it should feel warm and inviting. Now close your eyes and draw the image back into your heart chakra. Hold it close. Feel it; know it as part of your soul. Stay like this as long as you wish, then return to normal awareness and make notes of your experiences. You can reuse the invocation anytime you want to reconnect with that heart flame and invoke your rights as a cocreator in your destiny.

POWER SONGS

Power songs have roots in a wide variety of spiritual traditions, from the sacred chants of Buddhist monks to the shamanic healing songs of Native Americans. Such music has several functions. For one, it helps put the practitioner in touch with her own inner vibrations—those eternal patterns of the soul rather than everyday reality. For another, once a person finds her own song, it becomes a tool that encourages deeper levels of understanding and awareness, particularly in meditation. Over time, you can also learn how to direct this song to raise energy for various goals.

For this meditation, return to the world tree visualization. This time, however, the doorway into the tree will lead you immediately upward. When you can see that open doorway clearly in your mind's eye, open your magick mirror and move your spirit through.

Move slowly and steadily up through the world tree's branches until darkness surrounds you. It is not a frightening dark, but comforting like a warm cloak. The only things keeping you company here are the sound of your breathing and the beating of your heart. Pause here and breathe deeply of the silence. Still your soul and spirit, then look up and listen with both.

Near the top of your mirror you'll begin to see wisps of light, sparkling and happy. Far behind them, in the distance, music rings through the din. The sound is as old as time, yet as new as this very moment. Let yourself begin to hum with that sound, following along note for note. Keep repeating the melody until your whole body vibrates with the energy. (You may wish to have a tape recorder handy so you can listen to this later.) Release yourself wholly to the music until your voice naturally quiets.

Return to normal awareness, close your mirror, and make notes of your experience. The next time you feel your energy lagging or a sense of sadness or if you want to celebrate your spirit, start humming that song again. Also try using it as part of your scrying, as an adjunct to meditative efforts to deepen your trance state and when casting your Circles for ritual to increase the protective power therein.

REFLECTIVE RITUALS

The word *ritual* makes some people uncomfortable. They're reminded of lengthy church services, uncomfortable pews, and the seemingly unending drone of someone in the pulpit. Magickal ritual isn't like that, and you don't need a priest or priestess to enact one. For one thing, you are your own guru and guide in your spiritual life. For another, you already enact rituals every day without even knowing it.

Think of what you do first thing in the morning. What path do you take through the house? What cup do you use? What route do you follow to work? Do you see a definite pattern there? That's your ritual. Human nature seeks out pattern and coherency, so we naturally create mini-rituals in various mundane activities. This, in turn, provides us with a sense of dependability. Have you ever noticed that when something throws off your morning routine the whole day seems odd or off? That's because the pattern with which you're comfortable has been broken momentarily.

What is the difference between these mundane rituals and spiritual ones? Mainly intention. Magickal ritual acts like a blueprint that tells the Universe how you want your energy to manifest. Everything in and around that blueprint reflects the practitioner's goals. What might those goals be? Some rituals honor the divine, some offer gratitude for blessings, some invoke the powers for aid, some celebrate the seasons, and still others commemorate important human events like a marriage or the birth of a child. In short, ritual helps us fulfill our role as the priest or priestess in our lives and keeps open the line of communication between self, Higher Self, devas, and deity. And to my thinking, what better symbol of that open window than your mirror, your bridge between realities?

ritual constructs

Like everything else in a vision-filled tradition, there will always be someone, somewhere, ready to tell you how to enact ritual differently. Some schools of magick have precise protocols for ritual; others do not. Some work in a group setting; others do not. And some folks, like me, sometimes just fly by the seat of their broomstick and wing it when spontaneous needs arise. Is there a right or wrong to this? Absolutely not. But this does make it difficult to adequately explain successful ritual constructs to newer practitioners.

I would like to give you some ideas about what makes one ritual work and another flop. As with meditation, you'll want to try various parts of my recipe for success and see which ones bake up the perfect magick for your mirror rituals.

Think of ritual as if it were a living puzzle in which you have to put the pieces into the right places. These pieces can consist of actions like dancing, singing, chanting, drumming, casting spells, meditating, and ritual plays. The pieces can also be objects or decorative items like costumes, masks, candles, incense, ritual tools, and crystals. And don't forget one very important piece—you.

Before you even consider how to put together the key elements of your ritual, all these puzzle pieces should be properly prepared. This means that you should be rested and healthy and that any ritual objects you choose are properly cleansed. Magick always flows better through a pure vessel. If you're uncertain how to cleanse an item, some easy approaches include sprinkling it with lemon water or moving it through the smoke of a purgative incense like cedar or sage. If you have another way of caring for your magickal mirrors, stick with that (see chapter 1).

How do you go about putting the potential puzzle pieces together properly? That requires some thought. Take into account several things in designing a mirror ritual yourself, including:

❀ **When you want to hold it (and if special timing would be appropriate)**
❀ **Where you want to hold it (and any limitations that location may have, such as not allowing an open flame)**
❀ **The purpose of the ritual (the theme around which you'll choose the best puzzle pieces that symbolically support the magick's framework)**

Besides those considerations, rituals need an opening, a body, and an ending. How will you open the ritual so that you and all those participating can tune into sacred energies and put worldly thoughts behind? One common way is by creating sacred space (see the next section of this chapter). Other ways include prayer, candle lighting, meditation, and chanting.

The body of your ritual is what builds the energy. The actions that take place at this juncture are critical. As with spellcraft, if any action holds no real meaning for you, then it won't produce power. For example, if you're enacting a ritual to halt gossip, a lot of talking in the body of the ritual doesn't make sense. Rather, any spells or charms created at this point might be better done in silence, even as you want to silence the gossip. Again, it's coherency in thought (will) and action that counts here.

As for closing, this is the time during which participants switch back their awareness toward mundane things. Whatever happens at the closing should, well, provide closure. You want a sense that while the Circle is over, the magick continues. Some traditional parts of closing include dismissing the quarters, blowing out candles, and, in a group setting, saying something like "merry meet, merry part, and merry meet again."

The sample rituals that follow will give you a better idea of how rituals go together. Please read them over and personalize whatever you feel necessary to make the rite more meaningful and useful considering your goals. Or, use them as outlines into which you put all your own actions, words, and components. Remember, ritual is your mirror reflecting purpose and will to the All. You want that reflection to be as dimensional and specific as possible.

sacred space

Most magickal rituals take place in what's called sacred space. If you've ever walked into a church and felt an odd, holy hush fall over your heart and soul, you've experienced sacred space. Sacred space acts like a protective sphere between realities. Within that region you are beyond time and space. Here you can safely mix and mingling temporal and eternal energies (in other words, magick) and turn those energies toward the ritual's overall goal.

Creating sacred space typically consists of an invocation and visualization. In this case, we're going to add elemental mirrors (see chapter 1). An invocation calls upon the powers that inhabit specific regions of the Earth (North, South, East, West) to watch over and guide a ritual. Their energies combined create the protective shield around your space. Note, however, that this is an invitation, not a command. The elements are akin to demigods and thus deserve our respect.

To prepare, you'll want to have a surface on which to place the elemental mirrors safely (perhaps a stand as well, and a candle of an appropriate color like red for Fire, yellow for Air, blue for Water, and green for Earth). Most invocations begin in the East (the place of dawn) and proceed clockwise or sunward. The only exception to this comes when someone is doing a banishing or lessening ritual, at which time the invocation may be enacted counterclockwise or widdershins. The belief is that moving sunward inspires blessings, while moving counterclockwise unwinds a specific energy form (like stretching out a spring). Here's one example of an invocation (there are more in each ritual that follows):

East: Put the Air mirror with the reflective side turned outward away from you on the East-facing surface, light the candle (I usually keep this on the inside toward me), and say:

> *Powers of the East and Air*
> *I bring a bridge and open the way*
> *Come through this mirror to bless and protect this rite*
> *With winds of inspiration and hope.*

South: Place the Fire mirror similarly to the Air mirror on the South-facing surface. Light the candle there and say:

Powers of the South and Fire
I bring a bridge and open the way
Come through this mirror to bless and protect this rite
With the spark of enlightenment and magick.

West: Put the Water mirror on a surface in the West, light the candle there, and say:

Powers of the West and Water
I bring the bridge and open the way
Come through this mirror to bless and protect this rite
With waves of healing and creativity.

North: Place your mirror on a surface in the North, and light the candle, saying:

Powers of the North and Earth
I bring the bridge and open the way
Come through this mirror to bless and protect this rite
With soils of growth and firm foundations
So be it.

If you have made your mirrors with covers, you can lift the facing cover when you say "open the way" to improve the overall symbolic value of your invocation.

As part of the invocation, I like to place a mirror on the altar with a white candle to honor Spirit. How you create your spirit mirrors will likely vary on the image of deity you carry in your heart. I use a round mirror bearing an image of the eternity sign in the center so that it's generic. If you choose to use something like this, you'll want to place the mirror and light the candle on the altar after calling the northern quarter, and then say a prayer to welcome your deity. This last step helps bind all four elemental powers into a harmonious whole with Spirit as the figurative glue.

calling a familiar

A familiar is a living animal that has become a spiritual ally for the practitioner. Common familiars include cats, dogs, birds, lizards, and fish. If you do not have a familiar and wish to establish this kind of close relationship with an animal, this ritual allows you to send out a request for one. This request should not be made without thought. A familiar isn't merely a "pet"—this creature will become part of your heart and soul and work with you in magickal processes. A real investment of time and effort is necessary not only to make that initial connection but also to nurture it into a powerful partnership.

To prepare for the ritual, place your elemental mirrors at the four quarters and in front of them small tokens that somehow honor the elemental energy represented. For example, before Fire put some sand; before Earth, some rich soil; before Water, a cup of spring water; and before Air, a feather. The energies in these small tokens will be used to help disperse your request through the mirrors to the four quarters of creation, as you will see in the invocation. Place a Spirit mirror or your scrying mirror in the center of the room (on the altar if you have one).

PERSONAL PREPARATIONS

Look through some nature magazines that include all kinds of animals. What you get as a familiar can prove surprising, so try to release yourself from expectations. Just because you're a "dog person" doesn't mean your familiar will be a dog. When the call goes out, it goes to all elements, and when the right creature receives your message, it will appear.

THE INVOCATION

You should open your elemental mirrors as you recite their respective invocations:

> *East: Winds of communication, I call to you*
> *Across all space and time*
> *To join me in this sacred rite.*
> *Hail and be welcome.*

South: Fire of illumination, I call to you
From the fire in my spirit
To join me in this sacred rite.
Hail and be welcome.
West: Waters that touch on every shore, I call to you
across the water that is my blood
To join me in this sacred rite.
Hail and be welcome.
North: Soils of Earth, I call to you
From the land that is my home
To join me in this sacred rite.
Hail and be welcome.
Spirit: Breath of magick, Ancient One
Bind together these watchtowers in harmony
Of purpose. Come and bless my rite and guide
My energy.
Hail and be welcome.

BODY OF THE RITUAL

Stand before your altar or the Spirit mirror, which is already open. Using your own words, express your desire for a familiar and why this is your wish. When you're finished, move to the eastern mirror and pick up the feather. Fan it in front of your mouth as you come close to the mirror, saying:

If my familiar lives in the winds, bear to it my words and wishes.

Next, move to the South and pick up the sand. Sprinkle it over the mirror's surface, saying:

If my familiar is a creature of fire and heat, light its way to my home.

Move to the western mirror, sprinkling the water over its surface, saying:

If my familiar is a creature of water, let these drops guide its way to me.

Move to the northern mirror, sprinkling the soil on its surface, saying:

If my familiar is a creature of the forest or trees, carry my wish throughout the land so it can safely find its way.

When you're finished, sit quietly in your sacred space envisioning your home in as much detail as possible. See the doorway, the neighborhood, and anything that could be considered a nearby landmark. This is especially important if your familiar turns out to be a stray creature—this will help it find your doorway.

CLOSING THE CIRCLE

Walk silently to each of the four mirrors and close them; then stand in the center of the Circle, saying:

To the four corners of creation, I send my thanks and gratitude
When the time is right, bear to me my familiar
And help me bond with it in love and trust
Stay if you will, go if you must.
So mote it be.

Make notes after the ritual if you got any impressions from the quarter mirrors or from Spirit. Keep your eyes and ears open for that animal friend to make itself known in the days, weeks, and months ahead. If a long time (over six months) goes by without seeing a manifestation, you can redo this ritual and send out a second call.

shapeshifting

Shapeshifting is not what the movies would have you think. Unlike a werewolf, who is under a curse, this is a willful transformation of self that has a distinct purpose. Better still, it's an art that has ancient roots in shamanic traditions, among others.

The best way to describe shapeshifting is the donning of a new pattern. You can become a flower, an animal, a star, an element, or even another person. Although the pattern you're putting on is a reflection (which is where your mirror comes into this), it's a reflection that bears the same attributes and characteristics as the original. As you wear this reflection, you come into greater sympathy with it. In other words, you can learn from it and begin to develop some of those attributes and characteristics in yourself.

Although that sounds too difficult to learn, it's not. We do it already. Humans are natural mimics. Have you ever gone to another state or country and come home with an accent? That's a kind of logistical shapeshifting—your mind made specific transformations so you fit in better and felt more comfortable. All we're going to do now is apply that ability differently by making a conscious change for spiritual purposes.

PERSONAL PREPARATIONS

You need to decide what you want to become and why. For example, shapeshifting into a specific plant can teach you about the plant spirit's attributes and how to use it in your magick. Study images of what you wish to become so you can visualize it in great detail. Beyond this, it may help to use sensual cues. For example, if you're shapeshifting into a rose, burn rose incense and wear rose-colored clothing.

When setting up the sacred space, choose one mirror to be the center point of this activity. The mirror you choose should somehow represent your goals here. For example, if you're shapeshifting into a fish, you should use your Water mirror as the gateway. Simple candles at the four quarters are a nice touch for a visual sphere of light-safety.

INVOCATION

East: I would to welcome the winds
As they shift and change, so too the magick begins.
South: I would to welcome the fire

As it dances, so too energy moves higher.
West: I would to welcome the waves
As they fill a shape, so may my aura behave.
North: I would to welcome the earth
May in rich soils my magick birth.

BODY OF THE RITUAL

Get comfortable. If possible, pose yourself so your body shapes itself in some manner like that into which you're transforming. For example, if you're trying to become a dog to improve your connection with an animal companion, get down on all fours. Place your mirror where you can easily see it. Open the pathway to the world tree once more in both the mirror and your mind's eye.

As you stand outside the world tree, slowly shed your skin. See yourself simply as a being of light. It helps if you recall the heart flame of the god/dess meditation earlier this chapter and let that imagery grow into the full, nonphysical you. Move your spirit into the tree.

Bring to mind the image of the item you studied. Allow the details of that image to form on the surface of the mirror. When you see it there in full detail, begin to pour your light energy into that pattern. Remember, as light you have no boundaries. Your energy can adjust to whatever form you give it. The beauty of this approach is that you will get to know this new temporary house literally from inside out.

From this point forward, pay attention to all your senses and any other images that appear in your mirror. Continue until you start feeling weary, as if you can no longer hold that shape or image. When that happens, simply reverse the process, releasing your light energy from that shape and donning your natural skin once more. Take your time here. This activity often results in a bit of disorientation at first.

Ground yourself out and make detailed notes of your experiences to study in the days ahead. If you want to repeat the same activity with the same shape at a future time, you can. This will only add to your overall knowledge of that person or thing.

CLOSING THE RITUAL
Blow out the four quarter candles, saying:

> *North and South, East and West*
> *Thank you for all that you have blessed!*
> *Earth and Air, Fire and Sea*
> *Go on your way—blessed be!*

Next, go to your mirror. Speak words of thanks to the spirits of the middle realm that helped you with this activity; then close the mirror.

name quest

To know the true name of a thing is to have power over it, or such was the belief of the ancient mages. This is but one illustration of how much power names (and their meanings) hold in a spiritual setting. The importance of names is mirrored in temporal reality with various religious rituals that involve the giving or changing of names, such as marriage, birth, and induction into a religious order.

Your name can have a strong effect on your overall outlook and the energies in your life. If you don't believe me, watch what happens when you continually mangle or mispronounce someone's name. In a name quest, the purpose of the ritual is to unlock a name that's known only to you, the divine, and the elemental powers unless you choose to share it with others. This name may stay with you for a season to create a specific energy pattern in your life, or it may be yours for a lifetime, meaning it's part of your soul's legacy.

PERSONAL PREPARATIONS

I suggest not eating for at least three hours before enacting this ritual. If you can drink plenty of water and clear out your system a bit, do so. Also, take a ritual bath or shower so that your overall auric energy is as clean and natural as possible.

For the space itself, you can pick any mirror, but if you've been using your scrying mirror for world tree visualizations, that would be best. Being consistent in ritual protocol always improves the results. If you'd like to use elemental mirrors at the quarters, it's perfectly viable in this ritual as a way to open the elements for interacting with the ritual. Also bring a large white candle and a toothpick with you.

INVOCATION

East: Winds, I listen and seek your aid
Move to my ears with my true name
The one written on my spirit.
South: Fires, I look closely and seek your aid
Move to my eyes with my true name
The one written in the light of my soul.
West: Waters, I feel intently and seek your aid
Move to my heart with my true name
The one that flows with blood's beating.
North: Earth, I reach down and seek your aid
Move through my body with my true name
The one that resonates with every step I take.
Center: Ancient Ones, Guardians, Great Spirit
I stand between the planes
I travel the world tree seeking my name
Pray, welcome me in your presence
Aid my quest.
So be it.

BODY OF THE RITUAL

Set whatever mirror you've chosen central to your space. Begin walking slowly around it clockwise nine times. Each time you pass the surface of the mirror say: "I would like to know my true name." On each circuit, get closer and closer to the mirror. On the ninth turn, speak directly to its surface and open the mirror.

Sit comfortably in front of the mirror and take yourself to the upward entry of the world tree once more. You will be ascending to the top as you did to discover your power song. Once you reach that spot in your visualization, open your eyes, watch the mirror, and listen closely. Realize that your name may not be in any language you know or recognize; in fact, it could be a series of notes or sensations. Whatever you experience, repeat it to yourself so it becomes imprinted in your memory.

Take the candle you've brought with you and carve a representation of what you've discovered into your candle. Use letters or symbols, but focus on this name and bringing it into reality (the carving process helps with manifestation). Light the candle and speak the name into the flame three times. Claim it as your own. Feel the vibrations as they roll over your tongue and out toward the Universe. Turn and speak the name to your guardians and guides in the mirror. Gift those beings with your trust.

When you're finished, close the mirror, blow out the candle, and dismiss the quarters. You can light this candle anytime you feel lost in the crowd or when you feel the need to really get in touch with your inner self.

As you can see, I've kept the meditations and rituals in this chapter fairly short so they mix and mingle well with most people's hectic schedules. They don't require a lot of components, only your firm intention, will, and trust that your energy is being directed for the greatest good. Once you become more practiced with these, as well as with scrying and spellcraft, you can then add in tidbits of astrology and feng shui to augment your mirror magick efforts even further. Speaking of which, let's move along to those topics.

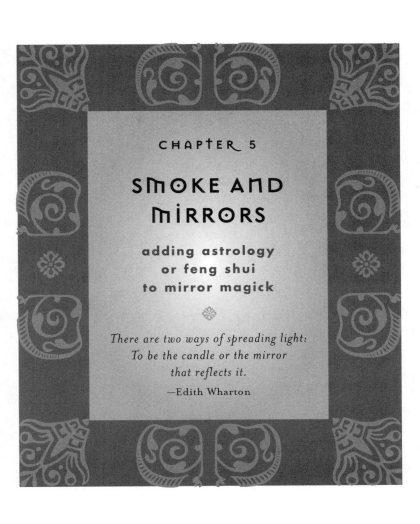

CHAPTER 5

SMOKE AND MIRRORS

adding astrology
or feng shui
to mirror magick

❧

There are two ways of spreading light:
To be the candle or the mirror
that reflects it.

—Edith Wharton

just when you think we've covered all the ways in which mirrors can participate as partners in your magick, something comes along as a wonderful surprise. In this case, it's using astrology and feng shui as adjuncts to what we've already reviewed or as stand-alone processes. In chapter 1, you began to understand the ways timing might affect your mirror making. Throughout chapters 2, 3, and 4 you saw how timing supports the focus of your mirror magick. So, looking to astrology as another option or addition makes perfect sense. And as for feng shui? By the time you get a feel for this system, you'll recognize its value as a wonderful and simple way of moving and manipulating energy. Since magick is to bend and change, feng shui mingles naturally and beautifully with metaphysical techniques. Let's start with feng shui since it's something many readers may be unfamiliar with.

FENG SHUI—GOIN' ROUND IN CIRCLES

Before discussing how mirrors are used in feng shui, it helps to understand the basics of this system. Once you're over that hump, it becomes much easier to adapt and apply it to both your mundane life and spiritual pursuits. In fact, since feng shui is as much a way of perceiving things as it is a method, it encourages balance between our daily life and our soulful adventures.

Let's start at the beginning—some 4,000 years ago in China. Here, what we commonly call the art of placement began as a system to inspire the best flow of energy (*chi*) for homes, buildings, and sacred spaces. In more modern vernacular, people were trying to manifest good vibrations that, in turn, encouraged long life, joy, prosperity, peace, and all those blessings human beings strive for.

To accomplish that lofty goal, feng shui practitioners begin by looking at a region (the landscape) to assess where the energy might be blocked. They divide any building or space into eight segments, based on the cardinal directions. Each of those eight points governs specific and unique types of energy. In turn, what's going on in that space naturally influences the way those vibrations play out in your daily life.

Let's look at one example to clarify this concept. Suppose your bathroom is located due north in your home. North is said to govern careers. If your job has "gone down the toilet," all of a sudden the reason for it becomes clear: the chi for your profession is being blocked or misdirected or has gotten out of kilter and needs to be remedied. Following feng shui guidelines, fixing this can take several forms. You might add the colors of black or blue to this region and hang (you guessed it) a mirror over the toilet to keep the energy from flowing down the drain.

These are the directions in the feng shui circle and their basic correspondences:

❀ **North: The financial region rules how successful you are in your chosen career as well as how you handle balancing work against your home life. This region contains strong nurturing energies. Colors: black and blue. Element: water.**

- ❀ **Northeast:** The Northeast rules over the conscious mind, theory, education, and learning new skills, including spiritual ones. Colors: yellow and brown. Element: earth.
- ❀ **East:** As in Wicca, the East is the region of beginnings and inception. The energy of this direction fosters kinship, steady personal growth, well-being, and improved vitality. Colors: pale blue and yellow-green. Element: wood.
- ❀ **Southeast:** This is where your abundance, comfort, and blessings lie along with your creative energy. This is an excellent region in which an artist should consider having a workstation. Colors: dark green and dark blue. Element: wood.
- ❀ **South:** This direction contains all the power of Fire, specifically the yang aspect, which controls your honor, courage, self-control, and the way in which others perceive you. Colors: vibrant red and purple. Element: fire.
- ❀ **Southwest:** This region rules over your luck, empathy, and relationships (specifically the peace and joy you achieve in personal interactions). Colors: rich brown and bright yellow. Element: earth.
- ❀ **West:** If you have children or pets (or anything you treat as a child, including pet projects), this region governs their fortune and future. Colors: white, gold, and silver. Element: metal.
- ❀ **Northwest:** This is what I consider the metaphorical help desk of your living space since it governs the cooperative and supportive people in your life. It also deals with the energy of service freely given and graciously received. Colors: white, silver, and gold. Element: metal.

Although this list is simplified, what comes to my attention immediately is that the West and Northwest may have the strongest resonance with mirrors and mirror magick because of the reflective connection (silver). And since making a magick mirror is a "pet project" in this book, either of these directions might be an ideal place to work during the construction phase.

Consider these correspondences in setting up your sacred spaces for spells, charms, rituals, and meditations. Move yourself or your mirror into the region where the chi best benefits your goals. If you wish, you can bring specially chosen candles into that space using the Eastern correspondences for their hues. Why use Eastern versus Western associations? Since we're working with feng shui, an Eastern methodology, the overall sympathy between your components and tools is strengthened if you stick to one system as opposed to mixing Eastern regional correspondences with Western color symbolism.

Here's a brief list of Eastern color correspondences:

- ❀ **Black: constructs, foundation, karmic law, deep understanding**
- ❀ **Blue: inventiveness, joy, inner beauty, wealth, kindness**
- ❀ **Gold: health, prosperity, power, universal wisdom**
- ❀ **Green: choices, determination, abundance, organization, health, sound advice, steady changes**
- ❀ **Indigo: ancestors, divinatory awareness, honoring customs, truth, discipline, honesty**
- ❀ **Orange: respect, safety, courage, certainty, wisdom, gentility, structure**

- Purple: inner peace, spiritual connectedness, fulfillment, authority, amity
- Red: passion, joy, love, ingenuity, spirit of adventure, overall energy or motion
- Yellow: stability, wishes, astuteness, sophistication, culture, friendship, safety from spiritual entities
- White: the soul, past lives, physical chi (yours), vanquishing darkness, journeys, youth

White can be used as a neutral, even as it is in Wicca, and the center of a room or space is neutral territory. So when you need to mingle a variety of the chi energies into your mirror magick, select white candles and place your altar in a central location.

it's elementary

In the correspondence list of the eight cardinal directions for feng shui, I included the respective elemental associations. Since these elements are a little different than those of Western magick, I'd like to take a moment to explain them in greater detail:

- Wood: Wood is the originator of the five-element cycle. It offers new life, creativity, socialization, and community-oriented energy. However, living wood is far better than processed wood for encouraging that energy. If having a living shrub or something else with a woody stem is not possible, substitute the color green. The Wood element is particularly helpful in overcoming anger and stress or for building strong partnerships and relationships. Wood's shape is tall, rectangular, or oblong. Water is the best companion element for Wood (as a source of nourishment).

❀ Fire: Fire is the ultimate yang (masculine nature) of feng shui. It's full of heat, happiness, cheer, enthusiasm, and activity. Some good options for improving the Fire energy in your living space include using red-colored light bulbs, sheer red window shades, or a red lampshade. Alternatively, a brazier for incense also works. Be careful, however, as too much Fire leads to "burning out." The shapes for Fire include anything triangular, pointed, diamond-shaped, or zigzag. Fire balances out too much Wood energy and can excite or evaporate Water energy.

❀ Earth: As one might anticipate, Earth has foundational, stabilizing, and nurturing qualities. It also represents the mountains, so many feng shui experts recommend rocks or boulders to balance out this element. Alternatively, clay statuary and potted plants will suffice. Earth helps ground out worry or angst and seems particularly helpful to teens. Earth's shape is the square. Earth gives Wood strong roots and accepts the energies of Water fairly well so long as it doesn't flood.

❀ Metal: Metal rules over businesses and personal success. It also seems particularly helpful for those trying to overcome sadness or grief. To bring more metal into your home, choose bronze or brass wall hangings and don't forget your silverware. Of course, the silvery tone of mirrors applies here. Metal is circular or oval. This works hand in hand with the feng shui mirrors that are typically oval. Metal is a good balance when there's too much Earth or Fire.

❀ **Water:** Water relates to travel, communication, learning, and the arts. It is also a clarifier that washes away fear and acts as a powerful protective force. Use simple fountains (metal or glass) and fish tanks to improve this element in your living space or anything colored blue or black that isn't associated with the Earth element. Water has no defined shape. Too much Earth cancels out Water.

As with all other parts of feng shui, balance, symmetry, and beauty among these elements are what bring about the best flow of chi.

I find it interesting that feng shui matches various hours of the day to specific elements in much the same way we pair zodiac signs with specific elements. Having this information may give you more ideas on when to enact a specific mirror methodology:

❀ **Wood:** 6 A.M. to 12 noon
❀ **Water:** 12 midnight to 3 A.M.
❀ **Metal:** 6 P.M. to 12 midnight
❀ **Earth:** 3 A.M. to 6 A.M.; 9 P.M. to 12 midnight
❀ **Fire:** 12 noon to 3 P.M.

the role of mirrors in feng shui

It's uncertain exactly how and when mirrors started being used in combination with the philosophies of feng shui. What we do know is that they appeared in China as early as 500 B.C.E., when small mirrors were attached to clothing as amulets against evil influences. Mirrors were often given as gifts to promote marital happiness and were buried with the dead with suitable magickal formulae recited. From ancient writings and associated lore, we can discern that even at this early moment in history the mirror bore the symbolic values of consciousness, awareness, water, connection between past and present, and the moon. Round mirrors were thought to represent the heavens and thus promote blessings.

A story dating back to the Ton Dynasty illustrates why mirrors are used in feng shui. In a province of China, a princess called Wen was married to a Tibetan prince. When Wen went to live in Tibet with her new husband, her father gave her various treasures as a dowry, including a magickal mirror. This mirror was beautiful, fashioned of two copper disks separated by a wooden frame and bearing a handle. Whenever the princess missed home, she could look into the mirror and see all the people and places she longed for.

The princess was accompanied on her journey by an ambassador who knew of the magick mirror. His mission was to ensure that the marriage went off flawlessly. So, worrying that Wen might become too homesick if she used the mirror, he snuck the precious item away and replaced it with an ordinary mirror. Of course, the first time Wen tried to use the mirror it did not work. She became enraged and threw the mirror at a mountain, where it split in two. One disk was exposed to moonlight, the other to sunlight. Two pagodas were built there in memory of the event.

With a heavy heart, the princess continued to Tibet. The marriage went well, and she was able to share Chinese culture, including Tantric Buddhism, with the Tibetan people. Today, to commemorate this story, sun-moon mirrors are still used to improve wishing energy (chi). The sun-moon mirror, however, is only one of several used in feng shui.

Another common mirror is called the Ba Gua, and it is a mirror of good fortune. There are three types of Ba Gua. The first is made of wood fashioned into an octagon four to six inches in diameter. The center of the octagon houses a two-inch mirror. The exterior of the mirror is painted in green, red, and gold to represent creativity, vitality, growth, productivity, and success.

The second Ba Gua mirror has a six-inch wooden frame holding an octagonal mirror. Plate glass painted with the yin-yang symbol covers the mirror. Typically, the border around the yin-yang sign bears four colors—blue, green, red, and yellow. The purpose of this design is to bring harmony to a room or a whole house.

The third Ba Gua mirror is made with wood that bears the scene of a god riding a tiger (a door god). This god holds a staff that keeps evil energies away and a plaque that declares good luck for all who abide in the home. These mirrors are often placed near doors to keep away unwanted guests, but they do not face out the door or the positive chi would simply be reflected away.

location, location, location

Knowing all this doesn't really help us in placing our personal mirrors correctly to help the flow of "good vibes." For that information, I turned to various feng shui experts, who often call mirrors the "aspirin" of this philosophy—they seem to be able to help nearly any imbalanced energy. Can you imagine calling your high priest or priestess and being told, "Take two mirrors and call me in the morning"? Well, in many cases, that's close to what feng shui prescribes.

Here are just a few suggestions for the best placement for mirrors in and around a room or home:

❁ Place a mirror near the center of a room, building, or altar to improve peace and good luck.
❁ Hang a mirror over a doorway to bless those who enter and deter negativity (this might also be nice for the figurative entryway of a Circle).
❁ Turn a mirror so it faces toward a source of negativity so it will reflect that energy away. In the Sacred Space, one might turn four mirrors (in the four directions) outward as a protective action.
❁ Avoid placing mirrors so you can see yourself in bed (it's thought to be unhealthy for the soul). This is especially important for people who have trouble sleeping or those just starting relationships. Instead, put the mirror behind the headboard where it can not only improve your rest but also help with struggling relationships.

- Place a mirror in a baby's play area. This helps expand awareness and increases personal development.
- Position mirrors in front of you, especially when your back must be positioned toward a door. This allows you to monitor the energy of each person who comes into your space. However, avoid having a mirror directly face the front door of an establishment, as it will reflect out positive chi each time the door opens.
- Place four mirrors on the inside walls of your garage and make sure the space is free of clutter. This allows you to leave road rage in the garage instead of taking that stress inside.
- Put four mirrors on the inside walls of sheds or other areas that have clutter. This keeps the chaotic energy of clutter away from your living space.
- In attics, mirrors should reside on the floor facing upward (take care no one steps on them), and for cellars put mirrors on the ceiling facing downward. This is doubly helpful if you feel either space is haunted by ghosts.
- Position one small mirror above the inside of your closet door facing into the closet. As with other cluttered areas, this keeps unwanted energy neatly inside and blesses your wardrobe. If you wish, hang a bundle of specially empowered herbs from the mirror for an aromatherapy appeal.
- If you have trouble in a particular area of your house, such as a bedroom in the North and difficulties with your budget, put a mirror in that area, facing out of the room so that chi reaches you more effectively.
- If you cannot work your magick in the most propitious room of the house for the need at hand, place a mirror directed

toward the area where you are able to work to take advantage of that extra energy.

- ❀ Stagger mirrors along long corridors or narrow halls, but don't have them facing each other. This makes the area feel wider and brighter and improves the flow of chi.
- ❀ Place a mirror on any door or window that is never opened to allow the positive chi to continue to flow and circulate freely.
- ❀ Oval mirrors bearing Chinese trigrams or other sacred symbols are thought to be the most effective. Mirrors that have been engraved are thought the least effective.
- ❀ Putting a mirror in a place where it gives a reflection of the stove and its burners brings prosperity and long life.
- ❀ Never place a mirror in such a way that it cuts off your head in the reflection. This brings bad luck and can cause sickness.
- ❀ Keep your mirrors and windows clean. This can improve your reception of daylight up to 30 percent (this is important for those who suffer from Seasonal Affective Disorder, also known as SAD). Metaphysically speaking, this also makes for a clear implement through which energy can flow unhindered.

expectations

Because feng shui is a relatively new concept to most Westerners, we're not quite sure what to expect from something that is both a philosophy and a methodology. My best advice is simply to focus on your goals. Trust fully in what you're doing. In both magick and feng shui, faith combined with mindful action makes a powerful partnership.

Quite honestly, to my mind, the greatest outcome from feng shui is a personal awareness that grows within the practitioner. Feng shui encourages a thoughtful, mindful approach to our living and working environments. Many of us spend eight or more hours daily in unhealthy spaces. Feng shui redirects our focus in those spaces and asks, "How can I fix it?"

Nonetheless, feng shui cannot wholly remedy those things that have been out of balance our entire lives or for many years—at least not quickly. This isn't a shake-and-bake, drive-through form of spirituality. Typically, there is a direct balance here. The more the amount of time and effort you give to it, the more it returns like for like. The harmony achieved by using feng shui combined with mirror magick slowly transforms negatives into positives and puts you back on the path of a happier, healthier existence.

Perhaps even more important than the externals is the shift that feng shui encourages in our soul. Even as you hang mirrors around your home for specific goals, don't forget to put the mirror of Spirit up to your heart and measure it regularly. Your body is the most important space you occupy. Whatever positive transformative work you do within naturally influences the externals in a positive, transformational way.

ASTROLOGY—IT'S IN THE STARS

Astrology is the great-great-grandparent of modern astronomy with a spiritual twist. This system of natural omen interpretation found expression around the world in various cultures and eras. In each setting, humankind looked to the stars and believed that something about them determined destiny.

The historical records of astronomy begin around 2000 B.C.E. in the region of Babylon. Tablets discovered in this region show that people felt divine beings moved celestial objects or created heavenly events in specific ways to illustrate a truth regarding the present or future. Within less than four hundred years over seven thousand astrological omens had been assembled into a collection for expert use.

Babylon wasn't alone. Mesopotamians, Greeks, Egyptians, Syrians, and Indians alike looked to various patterns in the sky, trusting that those patterns mirrored something of the divine will and workings. By around 300 B.C.E., the art of astrology was remarkably refined into the twelve houses we know today, with Aristotle leading the way in teaching applied methodologies. The Greek physician Galen (130–200 C.E.), along with other notable figures like Ptolemy, followed Aristotle's examples and expanded upon them.

It's important to realize, however, that the astrology of our ancestors differed from how we use the information today. Historically, astrology was more like a road map for travelers and a key to planting and harvesting seasons. Periodically, it was used to predict the outcome of important military maneuvers. But natal astrology didn't surface until 5 B.C.E., reappearing in 400 C.E., and it wasn't taken seriously until the early 1900s, when it became popularized by newspaper columns and farmer's almanacs featuring horoscopes and moon gardening suggestions. The word *horoscope* means "observer of time" (specifically your birth time).

Now people look to their horoscopes all the time for insights into various cycles and energies of the past, present, and future. The question for us becomes, how do we use the information astrology provides in terms of our mirror magick? I can think of several ways.

star light, star bright

I spoke briefly about wishing mirrors in the feng shui section of this chapter. Wishing is among the oldest forms of magick, and it's one you can blend with your mirror methods with little effort. You might time your wish spell or the creation of a mirrored wishing charm for when the first star appears in the sky. Make your wish on the star, open the mirror, and then recite the wish across the spheres.

Use this concept in the timing for creating amulets. In ancient times, Hebrew women of affluence used to have mirror amulets *(lehashim)* made for their clothing at auspicious astrological times. And while the practice was condemned as "magick," they wore them for protection nonetheless. If you create such an amulet as the first star appears at night, such an item would then protect your hopes and dreams and guide the energies of any previous wishcraft. Or, you could use the timing and energies of the zodiacal signs that follow to empower your mirror amulets.

sign, sign, everywhere a sign

As the moon and the Earth move through various zodiacal signs, the energy shifts and changes. Each of these shifts can be used as a support system for timing our mirror magick, as long as we know what signs generate what energies. Let's review the signs in the order in which they appear through the year:

❀ **Aquarius (January 21 to February 19):** Aquarius represents an adventurous spirit filled with idealism. When the moon isin Aquarius, this adventure turns into detached perspective sometimes combined with stress. When the sun is in Aquarius, the idealism is supported by real originality and clever approaches. This might be an excellent time to ponder the construction of your various magickal mirrors.

❀ **Pisces (February 20 to March 20):** Pisces represents kindness, empathy, and spirituality. When the moon is in Pisces, that empathy is strengthened by improved instincts. When the sun is in Pisces, the gentle spiritual nature is motivated by kindness and flexibility. This might be an excellent time to make magick mirrors for friends and loved ones.

❀ **Aries (March 21 to April 19):** Aries represents authority, leadership, and invention. When the moon is in Aries, that authority can take on a prideful air or gain some zeal. When the sun is in Aries, it provides strength for nearly any situation. This might be an excellent time to make protective mirrors or those intended to support self-confidence.

❀ **Taurus (April 20 to May 20):** Taurus represents a down-to-earth outlook and strong feminine energies as a counter to the masculine overtones of Aries. When the moon is in Taurus, it engenders devotion and resolve. The sun in Taurus generates faithfulness. Overall, this is an excellent sign when making or using mirrors to improve the quality of your relationships.

❀ **Gemini (May 21 to June 21):** Gemini represents energy often divided into two equally important directions, thus diversification is the key to balancing out this sign. When the moon is in Gemini, it provides insight. The sun in Gemini manifests with social energy. This might be the time during which you use your mirror for perspectives into your friendships (both good and bad) or when you're at a crossroad and need to make a decision (perhaps by scrying).

❀ **Cancer (June 22 to July 21):** Cancer represents long-term memory, shrewdness, economy, and an affinity for nature. The moon in Cancer creates a strong sense of dedication and prudence. The sun in Cancer tickles the creative yet cautious homebody. Cancer seems to be among the best signs during which to make mirror charms that protect your home and finances, as well as those that become gifts for remembrance.

❀ **Leo (July 22 to August 21):** Leo represents good luck, prosperity, and the enjoyment of material goods. The moon in Leo generates incredible charisma and passion. The sun in Leo sparks great courage. This is an excellent sign in which to make a sun or Fire mirror or a mirrored amulet to overcome fear.

❀ **Virgo (August 22 to September 22):** Virgo represents flexibility, keen wits, and a deeply reflective personality. The moon in Virgo makes things feel insecure, while the sun in Virgo provides rational energy and a strong sense of responsibility. Work with Virgo when your mirror magick is turning inward or when you want to support the conscious mind.

❀ **Libra (September 23 to October 22):** Libra represents good humor, adaptability, intelligence, and an overall sense of hospitality. The moon in Libra encourages courtesy and hospitality. The sun in Libra sparks harmony and inner beauty. Use these energies when you're working mirror magick for empowerment and confidence and when you need to be able to adapt quickly to changing circumstances.

❀ **Scorpio (October 23 to November 21):** Scorpio represents charm, strong emotions, and introspection. The moon in Scorpio brings an intense depth of feeling balanced with reservation. The sun in Scorpio creates determination. Overall, Scorpio couples best with mirror magick that's focused on heart issues.

❀ **Sagittarius (November 22 to December 21):** Sagittarius represents transformation, athletic ability, and pride. The moon in Sagittarius produces a surge of imagination and insight. The sun in Sagittarius liberates the spirit. Use these energies when opening astral windows in your mirror or when you want to manifest personal changes in unique ways.

❀ **Capricorn (December 22 to January 20):** Capricorn represents patience, strong convictions, and a sense for negotiation. The moon in Capricorn spurs sensitivity. The sun in Capricorn inspires practicality. Use this energy when you're looking to your mirror for insights and balance.

Since candle magick and mirror magick often go hand in hand, you may want to know the colors associated with each of these signs and then combine accordingly. Bright red or orange corresponds with Aries; dark green with Taurus; chestnut hues with Gemini; silver with Cancer; gold with Leo; variegated pastels or white with Virgo; sea green with Libra; vermilion with Scorpio; sky blue with Sagittarius; black with Capricorn; gray with Aquarius; and sea blue with Pisces. This information is useful not only if you want to add a candle to your astrological timing, but also if you cannot work during an auspicious phase. The candle can become a substitute for that time frame—blessed and charged items in the sacred space bear the same energies as that which they represent.

sign progression mirror

Chapter I discussed special timing for Cabbalistic mirrors. The discussion of the zodiac gave me another idea along these lines. What about a twelve-sided mirror with images of each sign etched into the frame? Here's an overview of the process:

1. Choose your frame material. Making the frame out of wood is easiest, but if you have metal etching tools or paints that adhere to metal, that base would be fine too.

2. This frame should be large enough to sit in a tabletop picture frame holder. Measure accordingly.

3. Using a router or similar tool, make a groove on the back of the frame in which the glass or mirror can sit.

4. Attach two small clips (like those you see on the back of picture frames). These will secure your mirror or glass so it doesn't fall out.

5. Have someone cut a piece of glass or a mirror that fits securely in the area you've prepared.

6. Treat the glass or mirror in whatever manner you choose from chapter 1. Set this aside.

7. Carve or etch the frame so the symbols for each sign adorn it as they might a clock's face, one sign on each of the twelve sides in their naturally occurring progression throughout the year.

8. Bless, charge, and energize your mirror in a manner befitting its function.

As each sign of the zodiac comes around annually, the mirror can be turned so that the image of that sign is at "noon." This honors the seasons and nature's cycles and makes a lovely centerpiece for any sacred space.

Make a personalized birth mirror instead of, or as a companion to, this one. In this instance, only the symbol for your birth sign would adorn the frame. These make excellent gift items too (especially on birthdays).

Finally, one last empowering touch you can give zodiacal mirrors is rubbing aromatic oil into the frame, which on wooden mirrors also serves to treat the wood and maintain the richness of the grain. Each sign of the zodiac has various herbs under its dominion. By rubbing these oils into the correct etched or carved sign, you bless the mirror with sympathetic and supportive power.

Better still, you can rub the oils into your candles too. Here's a list of zodiacal aromatics and juices:

- ❀ **Aries:** juniper, allspice, clove, ginger, marjoram
- ❀ **Taurus:** apple, cherry, peach, rose, cumin
- ❀ **Gemini:** dragon's blood, almond, lemongrass, mint, meadowsweet
- ❀ **Cancer:** balm, coconut, lemon, honeysuckle
- ❀ **Leo:** saffron, cinnamon, grapefruit, orange, rosemary, sage
- ❀ **Virgo:** lavender, celery, fennel, parsley
- ❀ **Libra:** verbena, apricot, mango, plum, raspberry, vervain
- ❀ **Scorpio:** basil, coriander, mustard, elderflower
- ❀ **Sagittarius:** dandelion juice, clove, coffee, tea
- ❀ **Capricorn:** cranberry, vinegar, beet juice
- ❀ **Aquarius:** anise, hazelnut, mulberry, sage, wisteria
- ❀ **Pisces:** clove, nutmeg, sassafras, star anise

east meets west

In China there's another version of astrology that is based on the year of one's birth rather than the month. While other factors (day and time) are also considered into how this birth timing is supposed to affect personality and one's fortune, the year is the main key for using this system. Each year has an animal designation that influences the energies anticipated in that year according to the animal's characteristics and attributes. There are twelve animal years altogether, and they cycle around as follows (both forward and backward in time):

ANIMAL	BIRTH YEAR
Rat	1972, 1984, 1996, 2008, 2020
Ox or Buffalo	1973, 1985, 1997, 2009, 2021
Tiger	1974, 1986, 1998, 2010, 2022
Cat or Hare	1975, 1987, 1999, 2011, 2023
Dragon	1976, 1988, 2000, 2012, 2024
Snake	1977, 1989, 2001, 2013, 2025
Horse	1978, 1990, 2002, 2014, 2026
Goat or Sheep	1979, 1991, 2003, 2015, 2027
Monkey	1980, 1992, 2004, 2016, 2028
Rooster	1981, 1993, 2005, 2017, 2029
Dog	1982, 1994, 2006, 2018, 2030
Boar or Pig	1983, 1995, 2007, 2019, 2031

Bear in mind that Chinese New Year is a little different than ours, so this doesn't match the Western calendar perfectly. We'll be going into the characteristics of each year, but here are the specific hours associated with animals to further refine your understanding:

Rat	II P.M. to I A.M.	Horse	II A.M. to I P.M.
Ox or Buffalo	I A.M. to 3 A.M.	Goat or Sheep	I P.M. to 3 P.M.
Tiger	3 A.M. to 5 A.M.	Monkey	3 P.M. to 5 P.M.
Cat or Hare	5 A.M. to 7 A.M.	Rooster	5 P.M. to 7 P.M.
Dragon	7 A.M. to 9 A.M.	Dog	7 P.M. to 9 P.M.
Snake	9 A.M. to II A.M.	Boar or Pig	9 P.M. to II P.M.

The Chinese lunar calendar is the longest chronological record in history, dating from 2637 B.C.E., when emperor Huang introduced the first cycle of the zodiac. Nonetheless, the exact origins of the twelve-animal system remain a mystery. Legend has it that the Jade King was bored, having nothing to do in Heaven. He could not look at what was happening on Earth, but he wanted to see the animals that inhabited his creation. His advisors were told to bring him twelve animals. The advisors first sent an invitation to the Rat, telling him to also bring the Cat. Unfortunately, the Rat's jealousy withheld the invitation from the Cat and kept it secret.

The remaining eleven invitations were sent on to the Ox, the Tiger, the Hare, the Dragon, the Snake, the Horse, the Goat, the Monkey, the Rooster, and the Dog. All animals were told to join the king in his palace the following day. When they lined up in front of the king, he found that they numbered only eleven instead of twelve as he had requested. The king sent his servant down to Earth to retrieve a twelfth animal. The servant ran into a man carrying a pig, which he hastily grabbed and delivered to the king.

The animals stood in front of the king. The Rat, being very small, hopped on the Ox's back and proceeded to play the flute. The king was impressed by this display. He gave the Rat first place in the order of procession. Second place was given to the Ox for being such a good sport, and third was given to the Tiger, who appeared so strong and courageous. The Hare was given fourth place, the Dragon fifth, the Snake sixth, the Horse seventh, the Goat eighth, the Monkey ninth, the Rooster tenth, and the Dog eleventh. By default, and because of the king's just nature, twelfth place went to the Pig. After the ceremony concluded, the Cat, who had found out about the Rat's concealment, begged the king to reconsider, but was told it was too late.

Like any good folktale, there are other versions of the story, some of which center around the Buddha. The Buddha sent out an invitation, and the animals that arrived and the order in which they arrived determined how the years were named. Thus, we find that a cat appears in some listings for the years instead of a rabbit. Other minor differences include a buffalo instead of an ox.

What does all this mean, and how can you use it in your mirror magick? If you know about each year's energies and how they affect you, you can then tailor your mirror magick (especially that for the Chinese New Year) so that it helps support or avoid specific situations. Here's a list of what to anticipate by year (forewarned is forearmed):

❀ **Year of the Rat:** During this year Rat has great fortune, Ox improves prosperity, Tiger stagnates, and Cat gets misled. Dragon experiences success in relationships and investments, Snake is very active, Horse has a bad business year, and Goat experiences financial loss. Monkey has success in just about everything, Dog is bored, and Boar finds victory with money and love.

❀ **Year of the Ox:** Rat works hard to stay ahead, Ox continues with prosperity that comes from hard work, Tiger must be wary, and Cat lands on its feet. Dragon has problems with other authority figures, Snake is working hard, Horse sees success in business, and Goat and Dog tuck their tails between their legs and just want to hide. Monkey and Rooster fare very well, and Boar needs to go with the flow and avoid anger.

❀ **Year of the Tiger:** Rat and Ox have a year of anxiety. Tiger finds its way to center stage, Cat wants some peace, and Dragon loves the hectic pace. Snake learns a lot (not always the fun way), Horse finds new pastures, while Goat feels wholly lost. Monkey is having great fun, Rooster would rather the sun didn't rise at all, Dog finds joy through devotion, and Boar faces numerous changes.

❀ **Year of the Cat:** Rat needs to watch its tail, Ox experiences improvements, Tiger can take a break and enjoy what it's earned, and Cat, of course, can enjoy life at its own pace. Dragon likes the overall energies of this year, Snake takes a sabbatical, Horse finds romance and jobs improving, and Goat finally experiences success at work. Monkey has good business prospects, Rooster needs to just recover from last year, Dog is content, and Boar is fine in all but legal affairs.

- ❀ **Year of the Dragon:** Rat has a pleasant year, Ox needs to be cautious especially with its dreams, Tiger gets lots of opportunities to show off, and Cat focuses on the home front. Dragon has a great year, Snake is peaceful, Horse finds satisfaction, and Goat and Monkey get a lot of play time. Rooster discovers a good mate or partnership, Dog needs a hermitage, and Boar want to stay close to its own.
- ❀ **Year of the Snake:** Rat contemplates and stays clear of business for its own good. Ox and Rooster alike have troubles at home, Tiger has wanderlust, and Cat has an overall good year. Dragon continues to shine alongside the "little dragon," the Snake who's having an amazing year. Horse finds love, but it's ill advised. Goat won't be bored, Monkey finds opportunities in abundance, Dog discovers new things, and Boar has a good year at work.
- ❀ **Year of the Horse:** Rat has numerous debts to handle, while Ox finds business success. Tiger has a new project, Cat has fun, and Dragon moves into a leadership position. Snake experiences disappointment in relationships, Horse has a lousy year, Goat has fun, and Monkey gets a great job. Rooster makes steady progress, Dog is restless, and Boar has the urge to organize everything.
- ❀ **Year of the Goat:** Rat recoups, Ox has setbacks, Tiger is on the verge of real troubles, and Cat experiences disappointments. Dragon shouldn't get overly involved, Horse begins to recover, Goat enjoys some personal growth, and Monkey is forever plotting. Rooster has no end of frustrations, Dog wants to give up, but Boar is hopeful and finally sees stability in both love and careers.
- ❀ **Year of the Monkey:** Rat is happy and moving forward, Ox has nothing but bad luck, Tiger's creativity surges, and Cat should pace itself. Dragon is wary of overexposure, Snake must find a coping mechanism, Horse reveals unusual political insights, and Goat returns to being a homebody. Monkey has an amazingly playful year, Rooster focuses on ethics, Dog

hurries too much and often experiences trouble because of it, and Boar has a fine year especially with relationships.

❋ **Year of the Rooster:** Rat's success continues, Ox gets back in the groove, Tiger becomes the rebel, and Cat is persnickety. Dragon should be cautious, Snake has a hard year, and both Horse and Boar have a great year at work. Goat should take some personal time off for R&R, Monkey has a slow-down, and Dog has many disappointments.

❋ **Year of the Dog:** Rat needs to look at its work and stay focused, while Ox is downright morose. Tiger has a good cause to chase, and Cat is feeling very wary. Dragon can do anything, Snake wants to make transitions but never quite gets around to them, Horse works for the joy of it, and Goat feels left out. Monkey has monetary restrictions, Dog has a fairly good year, and Boar keeps things quiet while improving financial stability.

❋ **Year of the Boar:** Rat should be looking forward and planning, while Ox should enjoy the lifting of dark clouds. Tiger is lucky, Cat finds contentment, Dragon has financial gains, and Snake is just trying to hang in there with the year's never-ending changes. Horse begins to realize dreams, Goat and Monkey also have profits, and Rooster manages only to maintain the bottom line. Dog seeks the comfort of home, while Boar becomes the financial wizard of the zodiac.

Let's put all this into a couple of examples. If you were born in the year of the Cat and it's turning toward the year of the Rat, you might use your mirror to improve your insights especially for seeing true. Similarly, Dragon might use a mirror this year as an aid in choosing sound investments since luck in that area is at hand.

You could also consider making a progressive animal-year mirror or a personal animal mirror much as those we discussed under Western astrology in this chapter. In making the personal mirror, bear in mind that the creation process invokes all the energies of your animal(s) and therefore will influence the ways in which you can ultimately use the finished tool. Here's a list of the traits and attributes for each animal:

- ❀ **Rat:** charming, aggressive, socially oriented, security conscious, honest, financially insightful
- ❀ **Ox:** quiet, patient, idealistic, somewhat temperamental or dogmatic, devoted mate, has strong work ethic
- ❀ **Tiger:** rebellious, idealistic, strong, generous, introspective
- ❀ **Cat:** upbeat, ambitious, refined, thirsty for knowledge, somewhat aloof, has good monetary sense
- ❀ **Dragon:** healthy, courageous, stubborn, blunt, emotional, demanding, smart, often talented
- ❀ **Snake:** wise, kind, humorous, charming, philosophical, tenacious, committed, sometimes possessive
- ❀ **Horse:** outgoing (especially in sports), happy, popular, driven by ambition, good with money but not with taking advice
- ❀ **Goat:** elegant, charming, good mannered, nature lover, procrastinator, curious about the supernatural
- ❀ **Monkey:** mischief maker, energetic, social, inventive, distractible, tends toward vanity
- ❀ **Rooster:** verbally aggressive, boldly honest, adventuresome
- ❀ **Dog:** dependable, devoted, alert, defensive, single-minded, detail oriented, worrier, hates injustice
- ❀ **Boar:** obliging, sincere, dutiful, strong, knowledge seeker, strong willed

If you want a mirror for glamoury spells and rituals, one dedicated to Rat or Snake makes sense. Similarly, if you want a special mirror for relationship-oriented magick, Dog and Ox make excellent options. Stretch your mirror magick in new, creative, and personalized ways.

*   *   *   *

IN CLOSING

When I started writing, I wondered how much information I could discover about one metaphysical tool. Needless to say, I was pleasantly surprised by the wealth of lore, history, and applications discovered. I hope you too have been surprised and inspired and will begin using mirrors in your magick in a variety of clever ways from this day forward. Polish them up and shine on.

MIRROR GODS AND GODDESSES

Speech is the mirror of the soul.
—Publilius Syrus (1st century B.C.E.)

In this appendix, I've limited the divine review to those beings who are directly associated with mirrors, not simply reflective surfaces like water. The purpose of this approach is to provide you with specific ideas about the Powers you could call upon to bless and support your mirror magick. Before you do so, however, there is one precaution. You should always come to understand a deity and build a relationship before inviting that Power into a magickal process or ritual circle.

If you view these beings as part of a greater One, or as individuals unto themselves, the power evoked in their names is not small by any means. A name has real energy, characteristics, and associated attributes that you or I may not be wholly aware of. Those aspects could really muck up a spell, charm, ritual, or meditation because the energies clash with your goals.

Also, I consider the Sacred as something worthy of respect and honor. Miss Manners says: One does not walk up to a stranger's door and say "gimme." Likewise, it's imprudent, if not downright rude, to metaphorically walk up to an unknown god or goddesses and ask for help.

Thus, I encourage you to take the time to research those gods and goddesses who seem to call to your mind and spirit. Learn about their myths and their place in their respective cultures. Find out what objects (flowers, aromas, animals, symbols) are sacred to them and put some of those items on the altar or in another note-worthy location. Meditate upon those beings. Open your mirror to them—talk a little; listen a lot. See if this is a relationship you wish to fully develop. If so, then move forward to integrating that being into your magick and life.

Al-Basir (Islamic): Another name for Allah, which means "all seer." Al-Basir is sometimes referred to as a universal mirror in Rumi's poetry.

Amaterasu (Japan): Shinto goddess of the sun and the initiator of the imperial family. It was a mirror that coaxed Amaterasu out of her cave after she was angered by the storm god, thus returning light and warmth to the world.

Aphrodite (Greek): Goddess of beauty often depicted in classical sculptures as holding a mirror.

Cerridwen (Celtic): Goddess of the cauldron of inspiration and rebirth—her mirror into the human soul.

Hawthor (Egypt): Goddess of beauty, whose face often adorned mirrors in that region.

Hela Barma (Buddhist): A white goddess. In her right hand she holds a divination arrow with a brass mirror attached. This is the tool with which she sees "all happenings in the three worlds and the three times." In her left hand she lifts a vessel filled with treasures. Peacock feathers are sacred to her.

Het-Hert (Egypt): Another name for Hawthor. Mirrors with Het-Hert's name inscribed upon them were used in an interesting ritual called a mirror dance from the Fifth Dynasty. This dance included a small sun disk—shaped clappers that were highly polished. As the danger was clapped, the percussion instrument would not only shine like a mirror, but also be reflected in mirrors. Clappers of this type were found in the tomb of King Tutankhamen.

Isdustaya (Asia): Goddess of fate who used spindles and mirrors to determine the future and each human's destiny.

Isis (Egyptian): Perhaps the most complete goddess of all history. One of her attributes is a mirror.

Krishna (India): Young women often sing a song to Krishna praying for mirrors that will provide them with wisdom. One story tells us that an artist was chastised for his attempt to paint a picture of Lord Krishna since the god has no fixed form and can change his face every second. Nonetheless, a wise person who knew this painter did not allow him to be discouraged and gave him the secret to capturing Krishna's true image moment to moment. Following the advice given, the painter again approached Krishna with something covered with a white cloth and told him that this time he was welcome to change in any manner but the painting would look exactly like him. When the cloth was removed, Krishna saw a mirror reproducing his exact likeness. The moral of this story was simply that a description of god will always fall short. The best you can do is become as a mirror to reflect that glory.

Kubaba (Asia Minor): Goddess of love. She has other names in neighboring regions, including Gubaba and Sauska. Her attributes include a mirror and a pomegranate.

Kybele (Phrygian): Originally a mountain goddess and the protectress of various towns. Her followers saw her as a goddess of nature and fertility who was often celebrated with ecstatic dance. Like Kubaba, her attributes were a mirror and a pomegranate

Mary (Christian): Mary, or Miriam, is strongly connected to a Hebrew root word meaning "mirror." This association didn't elude medieval monks. In the medieval Latin liturgy, Mary is called *speculum sine macula,* a spotless mirror.

Norns (Teutonic): Goddesses of fate often depicted standing around a three-cornered mirror.

Oshun (Brazil): Goddess of love and water who holds a mirror and a fan; the consort of the thunder god, Chango, and a deity of flirtation.

Tenma (Buddhist): Mountain goddesses and guardians of ledges to whom bronze mirrors were given in offerings.

Tezcatlipoca (Aztec): God of warriors, princes, and wizards. His name means "smoking mirror," alluding to his ability to see all things. In portraits he's shown with an obsidian mirror at the back of his head and under his feet (or replacing his feet). Although dance, music, song, and offerings were common to this deity, he was also portrayed as ruthless and cruel—the god of drought and famine as well as of warmth and life. The story goes that Tezcatlipoca was jealous of Quetzalcoatl's beauty and glory. He visited Quetzalcoatl and offered him a gift bundled in cotton. Quetzalcoatl unwrapped the gift, discovering a mirror. The god saw himself reflected in the mirror and for the first time realized that he had a human face. Being a god, he had believed he had no face, but now he began to think that perhaps he also had a human destiny. As a result of Tezcatlipoca's humorous gift, Quetzalcoatl drank heavily that night and committed incest with his sister. The next day he fled to the east on a raft of serpents, promising to return one day to see if men had taken care of the Earth.

Tipheret (Hebrew–Cabala): Deity of beauty, harmony, compassion, and mercy; also called the Lucid Mirror and the Sixth Sephira in the Tree of Life (see also YHWH).

Toshigami (Japan): God of the year, to whom mirror cakes are made on January 11 in a ritual known as "mirror opening," which encourages good fortune in the year ahead (see also Appendix B).

Venus (Rome): The emblem for this goddess was often a mirror, an attribute par excellence for the patroness of sacred prostitutes.

Vesta (Rome): Goddess of domestic matters; her celebrations were often opened by the lighting of fires produced by a special reflective glass or mirror held up to the sun.

Walbuga (Germanic): Weather goddess who seems somehow connected to the Wild Hunt. She is seen bearing a three-cornered mirror for seeing the future, carrying a spindle, and wearing golden shoes (perhaps an allusion to solar attributes).

Yesod (Hebrew-Cabala) Foundation: The "lower end" of the heavens and the pillar connecting heaven and earth; also called the seal of truth, the non-Lucid Mirror, and the procreative power; the Ninth Sephira of the Tree of Life. Note that the Tenth Sephira, Malkut (kingdom), also sometimes receives the designation of non-Lucid Mirror, probably because creation reflects deity but remotely.

YHWY (Jewish): There are allusions in the Old Testament to Moses using a luminous speculum (mirror) and a nonluminous speculum. The former is the clear mirror (Tipheret) through which only Moses could see, and the latter the dim mirror (Malkut) through which all other prophets could see.

MIRROR HOLIDAYS, FESTIVALS, CEREMONIES, AND RITUALS

We look into mirrors but we only see the effects of
our times on us—not our effects on others.
—Pearl Bailey

Mirrors are common implements in many civilizations. Their symbolic value, no matter the setting, is so strong that we discover a variety of holidays, festivals, ceremonies, and rituals that include this tool as part of the related activities for that event. This appendix explores just a few of these multicultural tidbits.

My purpose here is first to give you a greater appreciation for the diversity of ways in which people used something that we pretty much take for granted. Secondly, I believe that some of these events will give you ideas for other creative mirror activities and applications. You might use the date of a mirror-oriented festival for blessing your new magick mirror, for example. Or time a special scrying effort with a date known to support those energies. You might also find some of the methods in which mirrors were used applicable to a personal ritual or spell.

I do issue just a little bit of caution, however. As when you're working with the Sacred, other people's traditions should be adapted with respect and gentleness. Come to know the cultural context in which an event took place. Study a bit so you understand the full meaning of what a people did and, more important, why. From that foundation you can use or adapt the customs far more responsibly.

Children's Day (Buddhist): Corresponding to the Western winter solstice. Those celebrating Children's Day begin festivities by focusing rays of light with a mirror to start the fire and honor the sun. The central focus of the holiday is a specially built shrine with an indwelling king and queen. These may be special china dolls or statuary or even paper dolls. They are placed on the highest tier of the shrine as representatives of the heavens, along with offerings that depict each sense: a cloth ribbon (touch), fruit or sweets (taste), saffron water (smell), a conch or musical instrument (sound), and, last but not least, a small mirror (sight). This festival should not be confused with *Kodomo no hi,* another children's holiday, which falls on May 5.

Durga Puja (India): The basic aim of this celebration is to propitiate Shakti, the feminine aspect of the divine who can bestow wealth, auspiciousness, prosperity, and knowledge (both sacred and secular) on those whom she favors. On the tenth day of this festival, the images of the goddess are taken down and her reflection allowed to bless a large vessel of water. This is called mirror immersion, after which the water in the bowl is used anoint people to bless them with long life. In an alternative method, a mirror is adhered to a branch from an apple tree and placed so that it reflects the image of the goddess. It is then ritually washed to prepare the lady for her trip home.

Elusian Mysteries (Greece): Celebrated at the autumn equinox, this was a time for the faithful to deposit sacred objects at the feet of Demeter. Women carried baskets filled with the goddess's belongings, including a comb, a mirror, a snake figure, wheat, and barley, which were presented to the goddess. The women then bathed in the sea, put on new clothing, and poured out libations to the Earth. Finally, all gathered and celebrated in their best finery, dancing and shouting "Hail, Demeter!"

Enthronement Ceremony (Buddhist): This ritual is enacted upon the appointment of an abbot to a monastery, more specifically to recognize the incarnation of a rinpoche or to honor someone who has achieved the highest degree in Buddhist studies. Enthronement is believed to empower the abbot to carry out assigned tasks. The ceremony begins with monks offering prayers for the abbot's longevity and wishing him success in his work. Next, a senior lama begins the ritual by making an offering of the eight precious substances, which include vermilion dye, the white conch shell, medicine extracted from an elephant's brain, durva grass, bilva fruit, yogurt, white mustard seed, and, of course, a mirror. This is followed by a lesson surrounding dharma and the thirty-seven mandalas that help explain the offerings yet to come, including those of body, speech, and mind. Following this main ceremony, many precious things such as statues, brocades, and highly decorated mirrors are offered to the important guests and well-wishers.

Halloween (Celtic): On this ancient turning of the New Year (October 31), divination was a common practice. One custom recommended walking backward into a darkened room while looking into a mirror and eating an apple. If done correctly, you would see your future mate standing behind you in the reflection.

Hoi Gong Ceremony (Southern China): This ceremony signifies the birth into this world of a lion costume, specifically one meant to take part in the Taoist Lion Dance. At the beginning of the ceremony, the brand-new lion costume is laid out before a Taoist altar with the eyes and mouth locked in a closed position. The priest prays to the heavens for the gods to open the gates so that the lion's spirit may descend. Next, the costume is purified with the sprinkling of water using the leaf of a pomolo tree. Then, rooster blood marks the image of the mirror shield on the lion's forehead. This mirror shield protects anyone wearing the costume from evil spirits, who will see their own reflection and be scared away.

After the spirit has entered the lion costume's body, the eyes and mouth are opened. Small lights inside the lion's eyes are lit up to represent the presence of the religious spirit. Red paint is used to dot the lion's eyes so that the spirit can foresee good and evil. Finally, a red ribbon is tied around the lion's neck to represent honor and courage and as a gentle reminder to be guided by right and just action. This comes from a legend that says that the lion was once caught in an evil act. The punishment was to lose its head by the hands of the gods. However, the goddess of mercy felt that the lion had learned its lesson and put the lion's head back using a red ribbon to secure it. Therefore, when the lion costume awakens and pays respect to the gods, it bears the same red ribbon.

Initiation Ceremony of a Medicine Person (Mexico): Initiations typically take place on June 22 or 24. During this time, those attending (a number of people that are a multiple of three) seek after the wisdom of the fern root. This is akin to communing with a plant spirit, but it's considered most dangerous because the fern root opens the way to the underworld (meaning it has poisonous qualities). Thus, attendees are told to wear a mirror. As they reach the door of the underworld, directing the mirror toward the spirit that abides there will protect them and force the spirit to leave that door open for their return.

Jashn-e Arusi (Persian Wedding Ceremony): Just before sunset when a groom enters the home of his wife-to-be for the ceremony, the first thing he should see is the reflection of his bride in a mirror. This mirror, called *ayeneh-ye bakht,* or the mirror of fate, is provided by the groom beforehand. It's lit by two candelabra, one on either side, representing the bride and groom. These two things together, the mirror and candles, represent purity and love. In front of the mirror, the *sofreh-ye aqd,* a fine hand-sewn wedding cloth glittering with gold and silver threads, is spread out. Food and objects traditionally associated with marriage are arranged on it.

Kagami Biraki (Japan): This event takes place on the second Sunday in January. At this time special rice cakes known as *mochi* are offered to women's mirrors and men's armor and are also placed on the family altar. Besides this, some of the customary activities today include martial arts displays, students rededicating themselves to their arts, lectures, awards given by various *dojos* (schools), meditation, and special decorations for the god Toshigami, a deity of good harvests and prosperity.

Kagami Biraki translates as "mirror opening" or "rice cutting ceremony," and dates back to an old military custom that's tied to the three most important symbols of Japanese folklore: the mirror, the sword, and the sphere. Japanese legend tells of a deity who fell out of favor with the other gods because of his cruel nature. This deity was banished and eventually found his way to a secluded cave where he came upon a mirrorlike object. This mirror forced him to look at himself, reflect upon his actions, and try to discern the reasons why he was such a cruel individual. After many years of personal reflection, the deity returned to the other gods, who immediately noticed a great change in his mannerisms and character. This story was used regularly to illustrate the necessity of truthful self-reflection as a means for improvement.

Lantern Festival (China): On the fifteenth day of the first lunar month, *Yuanxiao Jie,* the Lantern Festival, takes place. In ancient times, young women and men did not have free social contact (it wasn't proper). The Lantern Festival became a perfect opportunity to look for marriage partners based on an old love story that, as you might suspect, includes a mirror playing matchmaker.

The story begins with two people, Huang and Wuniang, falling in love at the Lantern Festival. Wuniang feared her father would never approve. He was a greedy sort, and Huang decided there was a way that he could be with his love by using that greed against the father. Huang disguised himself as a tradesman who polished bronze mirrors. He went to Wuniang's home to polish the bronze mirrors and broke a mirror purposely. To pay for the mirror, he sold himself into the family as a slave. By doing so, he had the chance to meet Wuniang secretly. Eventually, they ran away and got married.

Navarathri (India): This Hindu celebration meaning "nine nights" begins on the day of the new moon and lasts until the ninth day of Ashvin (September and October). This is the most auspicious time on the Hindu calendar, akin to Yule in the Western hemisphere, and is thus accompanied by a great many activities throughout the land. The nine different aspects of Devi are worshipped over the nine days as follows: Durga, goddess beyond reach; Bhadrakali, the auspicious power of time; Amba, the mother of the world; Annapurna, the giver of food and plenty; Sarvamangala, the auspicious or luck goddess; Bhairavi, the power of death; Chandi, the wrathful goddess; Lalita, the playful goddess; and Bhavani, the giver of life. The festivities culminate on the tenth day, called Dussehra, when people in most parts of the country burn effigies of Ravana, Meghanatha, and Kumbhakarna (an evil king, his son, and his brother who were overcome by Rama after nine days of prayer). Among the traditional gifts for this period, we find turmeric, barley shoots, and mirrors (an attribute of Devi).

Shinto Purification Ritual (Japan): The purpose of the ritual is to restore harmony between individuals and their internal and external environment through purification. Before entering the temple, people remove their shoes and wash their hands and then sit on cushions on the floor. On the altar, offerings such as water, salt, rice, and wine are already set up. A round mirror, a holy symbol of the sun, is central to the rite.

The priest, vested in ritual dress, performs the ceremony with his back toward the congregation in the space in front of the altar. The ritual begins with an invocation of sorts, two bows, two claps, and one final bow. Attendees are sprinkled with water, and a blessing of reconciliation follows with the lighting of candles and invocations for the Kami (higher nature spirits). Once the Kami are invoked, the four directions are purified so that the environment resonates with harmony. At this stage, those present may offer a green twig as a symbol of peace and oneness. Finally, the Kami are released, and the ceremony ends with bowing and clapping (amen). At the end of the rite, the offerings, having been blessed by their time before the sun mirror, are shared among everyone present.

Shisha (Northern India): As part of betrothal and marriage rites, the art of *shisha* (a word meaning "mirror") became popular in Northern India some three hundred years ago. Women of lower class homes embroidered their garments and fabrics with tiny mirrors in an effort to emulate the luxurious clothing of the ruling class. Now this technique of embroidery is an important part of preparing for marriage and something in which all the women of a household typically take part as both a celebration and a time in which to exchange good advice for the couple.

Tea Ceremony (Japan): Every part of the tea ceremony in Japan is done with great ritualistic overtones and care. It takes years to master the ceremony, and one integral part is the pouring of the water. During this ceremony, the *hishaku* ladle measures out water to each cup. Next, the host holds the hishaku as if it were a mirror, in a position known as *kyogamae.* The host uses this moment to look into his soul to ensure that there is nothing within him to hinder his tranquility as he prepares to make the tea.

BIBLIOGRAPHY

Arrien, Angeles. *The Four-Fold Way.* San Francisco, Calif.: Harper
   San Francisco, 1993.

Barrett, Francis. *The Magus: A Complete System of Occult Philosophy.* York
   Beach, Maine: Samuel Weiser, 2000.

Budge, E. A. Wallis. *Amulets and Superstitions.* New York: Dover Publications, 1978.

Campbell, Joseph. *Historical Atlas of World Mythology,* 2 vols. New York: Harper
   and Row, 1988.

Cavendish, Richard. *A History of Magic.* New York: Taplinger Publishing Company,
   1979.

Cooper, J. C. *Illustrated Encyclopaedia of Traditional Symbols.* London, England:
   Thames & Hudson, 1978.

Fortune, Dion. *Psychic Self-Defense.* York Beach, Maine: Samuel Weiser, 1994.

Gordon, Stuart. *The Encyclopedia of Myths and Legends.* London, England:
   Headline Book Publishing, 1993.

Hawk, Ambrose. *Exploring Scrying.* Franklin Lakes, N.J.: New Page Books, 2001.

Hawkins, Holly Blue. *The Heart of the Circle.* Freedom, Calif.:
   The Crossing Press, 1999.

Jung, Carl. *Man and His Symbols.* New York: Doubleday, 1964.

Kunz, George Frederick. *Curious Lore of Precious Stones.* New York: Dover
   Publications, 1913.

Laurence, Theodore, ed. *The Parker Lifetime Treasury of Mystic and Occult Powers.*
West Nyack, N.Y.: Parker Publishing, 1982.

Leach, Maria, ed. *Folklore, Mythology, and Legend.* New York: Harper Collins
Publishing, 1984.

Leach, Marjorie. *Guide to the Gods.* Santa Barbara, Calif.: ABC Clio, Inc., 1992.

Lurker, Manfred. *Dictionary of Gods and Goddesses, Devils and Demons.* New York:
Routledge, 1995.

Monaghan, Patricia. *The Book of Goddesses and Heroines.* St. Paul, Minn.:
Llewellyn Publications, 1981.

New Larousse Encyclopedia of Mythology. Paris: Hamlyn Publishing Group, 1959.

Oesterley, W. O. E. *The Sacred Dance.* Brooklyn, N.Y.: Dance Horizons, 1923.

Tyson, Donald. *How to Make and Use a Magic Mirror.* Langly, B.C.: Phoenix
Publishing, 1995.

------. *Scrying for Beginners.* St. Paul, Minn.: Llewellyn Publications, 2003.

Walker, Barbara. *Women's Dictionary of Symbols and Sacred Objects.* San Francisco,
Calif.: Harper & Row, 1988.

Whitaker, Hazel. *Develop Your Psychic Ability.* Sydney, Australia: Lansdown
Publishing, 1999.

Zolar's Encyclopedia of Ancient and Forbidden Knowledge. N.Y.: Arco Publishing, 1984.

notes